ADVERTISING
IN EVERYDAY LIFE

THE HAMPTON PRESS COMMUNICATION SERIES
Popular Culture
John A. Lent, series editor

Advertising and Everyday Life
Neil Alperstein

Agent in the Agency: Media, Popular Culture, and Everyday Life in
America
Arthur Asa Berger

Jewish Jesters: A Study in American Popular Comedy
Arthur Asa Berger

Indian Popular Cinema: Industry, Ideology, and Consciousness
Manjunath Pendakur

forthcoming

Cartooning in Africa
John A. Lent (ed.)

Cartooning in Latin America
John A. Lent (ed.)

Serial Monogamy: Soap Opera, Lifespan, and the Gendered Politics of
Fantasy
Christine Scodari

ADVERTISING IN EVERYDAY LIFE

Neil M. Alperstein
LOYOLA COLLEGE

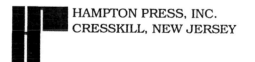

HAMPTON PRESS, INC.
CRESSKILL, NEW JERSEY

Printed in the United States of America

Library of Congress Cataloging-in-Publication Data

Alperstein, Neil M.
　　Advertising in everyday life / Neil M. Alperstein
　　　　p. cm. -- (The Hampton Press communication series. Popular culture)
　　Includes bibliographic references and index.
　　ISBN 1-57273-512-0 (cloth) -- ISBN 1-57273-513-9 (pbk.)
　　　　1. Advertising. I. Title. II. Series.

　　HF5823.A754　2003
　　659.1'042--dc21

　　　　　　　　　　　　　　　　　　　　　　　　2003051111

Hampton Press, Inc.
23 Broadway
Cresskill, NJ 07626

For Josh and Eric

CONTENTS

ACKNOWLEDGMENTS

Many people, over the course of several years, helped to further this project. I am forever indebted to the American Studies Program at the University of Maryland where I completed my graduate studies. In particular, the work of John Caughey enlightened me about the imaginary social world of the individual. I am indebted to Loyola College, where I have taught for the past 15 years, for the research grants and sabbatical—money and time—that helped support this project. And I am indebted to my colleagues at Loyola, in particular Barbara Vann of the Loyola College Sociology Department with whom over the past 5 years I collaborated on a series of research studies that were spawned by our common interest in the social world of dreams and dream recounting. Elliot King, a Loyola colleague, provided much support. There are many others who assisted me in this effort, too many to name, who played a significant role in the development of this book. I want to acknowledge the *Journal of Popular Culture, Journal of Advertising, Journal of Broadcasting and Electronic Media,* and *Communication Quarterly* where earlier versions of my research appeared. Finally, I am extremely grateful to John A. Lent, series editor at Hampton Press, who nurtured this project through to publication. I am most grateful to my students, neighbors, friends, family, and those strangers who let me into their lives to examine closely their thoughts, fantasies, and dreams in order to better understand advertising in everyday life.

PREFACE

Advertising is a luxury for U.S. business. It is a luxury because advertisers do not fully comprehend how advertising works to sell goods and services, and because the audience that is sold to advertisers as a demographic unit is neither unified nor controllable. Despite this dilemma, advertisers still spent more than $200 billion in 2001 on advertising that bought, by some estimates, exposure to 15,000 commercial messages each day.[1] It is interesting to consider why U.S. corporations would spend so much money on so many commercial messages directed at an audience that is misconceived as being everpresent in the light of advertisements.

Schudson (1984) said advertising's function is to legitimate differences between products, however, they rely on claims that may not be fully informative. Although incomplete in its presentation of information, advertising is pervasive in contemporary U.S. society. The key to understanding how advertising operates in the culture is through its incompleteness that opens up its text for multiple interpretations. Sometimes during the process of commercial consumption we may shield our eyes from its bright light; at other times we look at it through rose-colored glasses. As such, advertising is the site of an important economic struggle as well as a social and cultural struggle that is worthy of consideration. Beyond consumption of commercial media another struggle takes place: how advertising is used in everyday lives. Consumers may be socially empowered as they comply and resist the dominant position offered by advertisers. Storey (1993) concurred with this position when he suggested, "To deny that the consumers of popular culture are cultural dupes is not to deny that the culture industries seek to manipulate; but it is to deny that popular culture is little more than a degraded landscape of commercial and ideological manipulation, imposed from above in order to make profit and secure ideological control" (xv). In order to understand the meanings, pleasures, and imposition of ideology that consumers derive or succumb to through their interaction with advertising, a contextual approach that views advertising as "production in use" is essential (xv).

In U.S. commercial media there is an implicit understanding that in order to receive television or radio programming for free, and in order to reduce the cost of producing magazines, newspapers, and Web sites, advertising interrupts programs and editorial matter. The currency in this transaction is one's attention. In other words, a bargain is struck in which the individual agrees to pay attention to the advertising in exchange for the free programming or reduced cost of the magazine, newspaper, or Internet access. Advertising is the string attached to the "free gift" of commercial media, and it serves as a constant reminder that it is "you" to whom it wishes to speak. If advertising worked the way the industry would like, individuals would not have time to watch, read, or listen to the commercial messages, as they would spend all of their time shopping. But the truth is, people do not spend all of their time shopping; advertising's effects are limited.

Andrew Robertson, president and chief executive at BBDO North America, referred to the 21st century as being about "the attention economy." The media may be pervasive in their reach, he said, but getting people to pay attention is of prime concern to advertisers. Robertson said the goal of advertising is to develop "that magical ability to capture and hold and engage somebody's attention." (Elliot, 2001: C8). Despite the millions of dollars that is spent each year on consumer research, little is known about the way in which individuals operate within the magical world of advertising. Yes, it is true that people may pay little or no attention to advertising. But sometimes they pay partial attention to it. And, yet other times they pay direct attention to it, but mangle the message. Finally, sometimes, under some circumstances, some consumers actually purchase (for various reasons) the products they see advertised.

The subject of this book goes beyond the traditional cause-and-effect relationship between advertiser and consumer to explore some of the work advertising does in the culture—advertising's magic—and the work we do with it. When I refer to the *work* of advertising in the culture, I am concerned with how the "text" of advertisements operates within the uneven and variable social "context" of everyday life. The site of investigation is media consumption—watching television, reading magazines, and so on. But the investigation extends beyond media consumption to include routine practices like eating breakfast, attending a dinner party, or hanging out at the local shopping mall, among others. The task set forth, as Carey (1998) described it, "like that of a literary critic, is to interpret the interpretations" of consumers' routine practices (60). I am less concerned with demographics and psychographics as these are means by which the industry attempts to tame the wily beast (audience). I am, however, vitally concerned with observing human action and interaction—advertising as a social practice. It is my contention that the *work* individuals do with advertising is quite independent of demographic constraints, as individuals are active participants in the game of advertising.

During the 1920s, known as the age of salesmanship, the advertising industry began to be popularly referred to as the *ad game.* In contemporary society, advertising has been transformed into a cat and mouse game where the advertisers are constantly chasing consumers, not only during media consumption. Consumers are bombarded with advertisements on taxis, buses, signs, and teeshirts, just to name a few alternative media that become the background of daily life. Advertising has become an integral part of the U.S. landscape. In the same way that it papers the walls of society, it also enters our daydreams, night dreams, and the social discourse of everyday life. And like most games, sometimes we get "caught," but other times we escape to play another day. The game of advertising is not fatal, but it does impinge on aspects of everyday life that have not been closely examined. The question as to whether advertising adds value to everyday life, I leave to the reader to decide. However, I reject the idea that audiences are cultural dupes waiting to be taken in by the manipulative practices of advertising. At the same time, recalling that contradictory forces are at work, I do not conceive of the audience as so removed as to be immune from the cultural and perhaps financial imposition of advertising. Rather, I advance the idea that advertising is a power to be reckoned with, a hegemonic force in the culture and society. But once confronted by advertising, it is interesting to see what individuals do with it. That is what this book is primarily about—what individuals do with advertising in the context of their everyday lives. And although I may not be able to fully answer that question regarding what they do with it, the main purpose of this book is to better understand advertising's text in the context of everyday American life.

As I considered the topic for this book, I wanted to go beyond the notions of passive or active audiences and to locate the subject, advertising, in the natural world of the individual. When I began to research advertising in the late 1980s, I sought to locate advertising "texts" in various social contexts and to look at the struggle that ensued when the two collided. Bombarded by so many commercial

messages, advertising whether we like it or not, is a part of our ordinary existence. And as such, our engagement with it or avoidance of it
is a routine social practice. The nature of that engagement with advertising is the centerpiece of this book.

Humanistic inquiry does not fit squarely into the positivist science of much advertising research. Everyday life studies deal with the
commonplace, the ordinary; things we take for granted. This is no less
so for mass media and in that, advertising that have become integrally
ingrained in everyday American life. Advertising is a part of our everyday existence and remains to a great extent unnoticed like other routines of daily life. This book aims to further the ethnographic understanding of advertising as a social practice. Perhaps because of its
ubiquity, advertising does not get scrutinized in a way that renders its
social utility transparent for critical analysis. It does require getting
close to your subject in order to render the subtle nature of routine
behaviors or cultural practices apparent. Like brushing one's teeth, the
use of advertising is an experience often taken for granted—that is how
culture works.

The ethnographic approaches utilized in this book provide a
micro-view of the particularities of everyday American life. I have studied the kinds of consumptive practices that yield a diverse set of experiences with and through advertising. In particular, I have observed the
social world of the individual and unveiled the ways in which advertising circulates through it, via the individual's stream of consciousness,
including daydreams and fantasies, night dreams, and imaginary
social relationships that are inhabited by media figures. I hope this
book furthers the understanding of humanistic methods for studying
advertising audiences. The cultural theory advanced in this book is not
meant to be holistic, and therefore offers a partial explanation regarding the place and purpose of advertising in U.S. culture and society.

In Part I I provide a broad framework for understanding advertising in U.S. culture. Chapter 1 explores the political positions that
have led to the critique of advertising. With the critique as background,
I begin to lay the groundwork for understanding advertising within the
culture; in particular, this chapter introduces the concept of advertising as a social practice. Advertising as a social practice is a concept
rooted in the work of de Certeau who was concerned with the creative
ways in which individuals make culture within the routine practices of
everyday life. Chapter 2 examines advertising's roots in the religious
Carnival and market fairs of the early modern period. The chapter suggests that the carnivalesque qualities of the fair exist today within the
magical qualities of contemporary advertising. I present the idea that
advertising serves as a replacement for the tactility of goods. The
abstraction of goods as detached from the process of labor and production is something Marx described as a condition of capitalism. In this

chapter I also examine the volatile market forces that advertisers seek to control; forces that become part of our meaning-making system through which we experience advertising's magic.

Part II presents a series of empirical studies of the uses of advertising in everyday life. Chapter 3 explores the thoughts—stream of consciousness and fantasy—consumers engage in when they are consuming advertising. Beyond the stream of consciousness, the chapter explores the self-talk individuals engage in as they attempt to make sense of their world and the advertisements they have just seen or read. The stream is like a "mental commercial," an opportunity to take a break from the commercial break. When one engages in a mental commercial one enters an imaginary social world that parallels the actual world of the individual. The first part of Chapter 4 further examines the imaginary world of the individual with particular regard for dreams about advertising, media figures, and advertised products and services. The second part of the chapter is concerned with the sharing of dreams and how products and other advertising-related material, as part of the social utility of advertising, does and does not present itself in the course of sharing dreams with others. Chapter 5 explores the imaginary social relationships consumers have with media figures appearing in advertisements. This extends the work on imaginary social worlds, a pervasive form of pseudosocial interaction. We know more media figures than actual people, and when some of those media figures are present in advertisements the imaginary relationship is sometimes enhanced, but also may be altered. Consumers use their experience with the media figure's appearance in advertising as a means to make sense of the relationship, the advertisement, and perhaps they use the media figure to help evaluate something about the product or service being advertised. The final chapter of Part II explores the ways in which the content of advertising circulates through American culture. The circulation of advertising content in everyday life is a social practice that amplifies advertising's role in the culture. This social practice that takes place within the ordinariness of everyday life is quite complex and suggests how the elements of advertisements—catch phrases, slogans, and the like—jump off the page or screen and sometimes enter social discourse.

Part III is concerned with the significance of advertising in American culture and presents a means by which to understand its paradoxical nature. Chapter 7 provides a broad summary of the research presented in the previous section. The chapter describes the cultural significance of advertising within the variety and range of uses that consumers employ. The chapter does not conceive of the consumer as either powerful or powerless, but as a player in the game of advertising where there sometimes are opportunities to be subject to its power, but other times to invoke its contents on our own behalf.

The final chapter presents a partial theory of advertising in everyday life. The chapter describes a continuum of meaning on which advertising operates. This continuum considers that advertisements sometimes are meaningful, but are at other times meaningless. The continuum is not a set of fixed points, but rather a somewhat chaotic matrix in which advertisers attempt to create meaning or experiences while consumers sometime fix on the intended meaning, but at other times they may unmake or remake that meaning. The process operates like a moving equilibrium, or to put it more simply, like a cat and mouse game.

ENDNOTES

1. See Berger (2000), in which he reported this figure as an estimate of daily advertising exposure from all sources.

PART I

1

ADVERTISING
AS A SOCIAL PRACTICE

Advertising has been a part of the U.S. landscape since the beginnings of the country, although, there has always been much ambivalence about its role in society. Interest in and inquiry into advertising in America dates to 1759 when Dr. Samuel Johnson, literary titan of the 18th century suggested, "advertisers had moral and social questions to consider" (Aaker & Day, 1978, p. 174). Since that time, the institution of advertising has played an increasingly significant role in the financial and cultural economies.

This chapter begins with a discussion of the ideological positions—liberal, Marxist, and conservative—regarding advertising. Understanding these positions will ground advertising's role in the financial as well as the cultural economy. The cultural role of advertising in everyday life is explored along with audience reception of advertising messages. The social uses in advertising are described and the concept of advertising as a social practice is introduced.

Advertising as we know it is a 19th-century phenomenon. In the latter part of the century, national consumer product advertising arose as an economic necessity as modern society progressed from a competitive economy to an oligopoly. With fewer producers, the excesses of production needed to be widely distributed and advertising was the vehicle with which to stimulate demand among consumers to ensure that the goods produced in large numbers would be eliminated from inventories, and to ensure that the owners of the factories producing them could secure adequate returns on their investments. Fox (1984) and Lears (1994) described this process of commodification and the social structure that emerged as "consumer culture," an idealized vision of 20th-century life. Ewen and Ewen (1982) also found during this period similar growth in consumer culture through the rise of mass images, fostered by the fashion and entertainment industries. As advertising replaced traditional means of conveying information its importance grew as a social power along with its ability to set a cultural tone with regard to image and lifestyle. The focus on advertising as a social and cultural power emerged over the course of the 20th century as theorists and critics came to describe the rise of goods and services as signifiers of status in addition to their role in needs gratification.

SOCIAL CRITIQUE OF ADVERTISING

Paralleling the growth of advertising during the 20th century, as the consumer economy emerged, was an economic and social critique of advertising. Liberal critics believe the economic impact of advertising is wasteful, and therefore, it should be eliminated. Such critics believe that advertising creates barriers to entry into the marketplace and thus decreases competition. This, they say, leads to oligopolies. Additionally, the liberal position maintains that advertising is an inefficient conveyor of information, distributing information unevenly. This inefficiency and unevenness leads to an increase in prices because the sum total of advertising must be absorbed into the cost of doing business. With regard to social impact, the liberal position maintains that by placating an individual's wants, advertising maintains the status quo. Other ways in which advertising impacts society from the liberal perspective include creating false wants, presenting bad role models, and affecting programming content adversely.

Leiss, Kline, and Jhally (1986) suggested that the neoliberal and Marxist positions toward advertising are quite similar. The neoliberal and Marxist critique is based on the idea that advertising is a tool of manipulation that controls the market by creating false needs in consumers and by extolling an ethos of consumption. The neoliberal critique overemphasizes the idea that consumption fulfills all needs through the purchase of goods in the marketplace. As all of these needs cannot be fulfilled through consumption, according to the critique, general feelings of dissatisfaction emerge. But neoliberals believe that advertising can be "fixed" through the containment of market forces. This can be accomplished through public policy and government action.

The conservative critique claims that advertising leads to a moral breakdown of society as it foists images of hedonistic pleasure on an unsuspecting public. The conservative position, that politically represents the religious right, criticizes advertising as a celebration of secular humanism.

The critique of advertising in its various manifestations progressed through the 1950s and 1960s. Historian David Potter, for example, proclaimed advertising to be the dominant institution in American society. Potter (1954) claimed for advertising as much influence as the institutions of religion and education, and ascribes to advertising the "power to exhibit social control by shaping popular standards" (166). In the late 1950s, Packard's *Hidden Persuaders* popularized this critical stance, introducing the concept of subliminal advertising to the popular lexicon. Even though there is little scientific evidence to support the notion of subliminal advertising and little reason for advertisers to engage in it, Americans are steadfast in their belief in its existence and hence their belief in the magical forces of advertising. And, Toynbee (1964), during this same period, attacked advertising and its effects on values in American culture and society:

> The true end of man is not to possess the maximum amount of consumer goods per head. When we are considering the demand for consumer goods we have to distinguish between three things; our needs, our wants and the unwanted demand, in excess of our genuine wants, that allow the advertising trade to bully us into demanding if we are both rich enough to let ourselves be influenced by advertisements. (144)

In the decades that followed, the rhetoric has been just as strong. Boorstin believes that advertising is the rhetoric of democracy and an important element in understanding American civilization. Real (1977) described advertising's manifest function as conveyor of information to consumers about goods and services, but he adds it does so in the context of "a world of fables, morality plays, reflections of power and priorities in our society" (28).

Leiss et al. (1986) conceptualize advertising as an influential form of social communication.

> Our main point is a simple one: Advertising is not just a business expenditure undertaken in hope of moving some merchandise off the store shelves, but is rather an integral part of modern culture. Its creations appropriate and transform a vast range of symbols and ideas; its unsurpassed communicative powers recycle cultural models and references back through the networks of social interactions. This venture is unified by the discourse through and about objects, which bonds together images of persons, products, and well-being (7).

Their concern is for the significance and power of advertising as a purveyor—not of goods and services—of culture. They claim for advertising
a crucial role in the culture's meaning-making system.

Perhaps because of its complex role—it is entertaining, supports the media system, and serves as an engine for commerce—this
love/hate relationship continues today as advertising is still being
referred to as the central institution of American culture (Twitchell,
1996). This love/hate relationship with advertising is rather paradoxical, especially when it comes to the effectiveness of advertising. In a
fragmented society advertising reaches a diverse nation through target
marketing's appeals to various tastes. This narrow casting of advertising's net takes advantage of multiple, yet highly fragmented, media
outlets. The audience to which it is directed is diverse and difficult to
control. And, the message through which it makes offers is constructed
within highly fractured forms.

Most people, however, "hold simultaneously divergent, indeed
opposed, views on advertising" (Leiss et al., 1986: 4). This divergence of
opinion is reflective of society as a whole and thus our understanding
of the place and purpose of advertising within American culture is not
a particularly clear one. Nevertheless, advertising, like the mass media
of which it is a part, is fodder for controversy and criticism. We have
come to have a complex relationship with advertising as it is intertwined within the financial economy serving to support the capitalist
system, and within the cultural economy where it weighs heavy on the
issues regarding values, morals, obtrusiveness, intrusiveness, and
deceptiveness.

COMING TO TERMS WITH THE CRITIQUE

Advertising competes with other institutions—political, economic, and
social—for a place in public discourse and within the private imagination. In order to dominate the culture, advertisements have to be more
compelling and encompassing in their appeals than those communi-
cated through other institutions. Sometimes, of course, advertisements
do for a short time rise to the level of prominence. Sometimes when an
advertisement does so the reasons have little do with the product per
se, and have more to do with the context of the advertisement and
related issues: Joe Camel and youthful smokers, fashion and drug
abuse, and fashion models and child abuse, just to name a few.
Conversely, it may be that other topics—news, entertainment, and so
on—may at a point in time lack salience providing the opportunity for
advertising to take a more prominent position in popular culture. From
time to time advertising becomes news, for example, when pop singer

Michael Jackson's hair caught fire while filming a Pepsi commercial. Fowles (1996) described advertising and popular culture as "allied symbol domains" (xiv).

The inability to commandeer all the media or to create messages that reach a diverse culture suggests that we do not live in an age dominated by advertising. Advertisements lack the ability to reach all of the people all of the time even though oftentimes it feels as though we are inundated by commercial messages. In order to be considered a dominant institution, advertising would have to do more than bombard consumers with images and messages, and consumers would have to actually pay attention, internalize the messages, and perhaps act on those messages and images.

Advertising is more like a re-packager of cultural artifacts rather than an originator of culture. "The advertisement does not so much invent social values or ideals of its own as it borrows, usurps, or exploits what advertisers take to be prevailing social values" (Schudson, 1984: 221). This is so because advertising to some degree reflects the culture of which it is a part. Furthermore, advertising does not directly reflect the culture accurately as it represents a refracted picture of society. Rather than reality, advertising presents to its audiences a form of hyper-reality; an extension of reality that manifests in excessiveness. There is a solipsistic quality to advertising as it does not so much create culture, but it is a product of the culture that feeds culture back into the culture. And because we live in a diverse society, this combination of refracted images projecting the excessiveness of advertising through highly fragmented media sets up the possibility that the interpretations and uses of advertising will be various and wide ranging.

In this same sense, advertising rarely offers anything new, but relies on fracturing readily understood forms in order to gain attention. As there is little economic incentive in being overly risky, generally speaking, advertisers choose not to lead the culture. Advertising campaigns by Calvin Klein and Benneton, for example, have sometimes intentionally heightened social contexts in an attempt to tag their brand name to a social issue in the foreground.[1] Benneton did not originate the social issue of death row inmates who served as background for a recent campaign; they did tag onto the issue and heighten for a short time public awareness of the issue. The primary focus of such advertising, however, is not on products sold by the advertiser. Therefore, the range of possible interpretations grows within this complexity. Once unleashed on the culture, can an offensive advertisement—that mixes high fashion sweaters, as is the case with Benneton, and a public issue like the death penalty—work in the controlled manner in which the marketer desires? If the goal is to raise awareness of the brand, perhaps so, but if the goal is to encourage individuals to purchase Benneton fashions, then the answer is caught in the intertextual nature of advertising as it operates within a complex set of social and cultural rules.

Additionally, culture is not static, but rather changes over time. Accordingly, advertising being a product of the culture, over time, changes too. As advertising reflects, or rather refracts, part of the culture it is not one thing over a long period of time; it has a dynamic, yet synergistic, quality. And so under some circumstances, some times, for some individuals advertising, or more likely certain aspects of it, may be relevant. The possible outcomes range from purchasing a product to utilizing a catch phrase in some social situation. However, individuals may pay little or perhaps no attention to advertising, what Krugman (1988) called *learned inattention*. To understand the purpose and place of advertising in American culture, it is important to look more deeply at the variety and range of experiences individuals have with and through advertising, social practices in everyday life.

ADVERTISING AND THE SALE OF PRODUCTS

Advertising operates within both the cultural and financial economies. Considering the inability to measure its effectiveness within the financial economy, it has always been difficult to judge the contribution advertising makes to the bottom line of an organization. This is so if for no other reason than for many companies, sales figures are proprietary information, not shared with the general public, and it is difficult to demonstrate a causal relationship between what we see, read, or hear and ensuing behavior. Driver and Foxall (1984), in their review of the advertising literature, concluded "advertising is helpless when it comes to establishing long-term purchasing patterns" (in Leiss et al. 1986: 5). Leiss et al. amplified this point when they said, "Historical analysis has been unable to determine just how much advertising, as distinct from other factors, increased overall sales and stimulated mass production and distribution. The growth of advertising is correlated to the growth of the industrial economy, but whether as cause or effect is difficult to determine" (14).

Part of the problem with correlating advertising effectiveness and sales is the lack of differentiation between categories such as national consumer goods, retail, business, and professional advertising. There is also confusion regarding the difference between advertising, sales promotions, and direct marketing efforts and the different goals of each. Generally, we accept the term *advertising* to mean any attempt to "sell" a product on behalf of a purveyor. This would include a promotional event, like the Super Bowl, and it might include coupons consumers receive in the mail or those inserted into a Sunday newspaper. It might include an advertisement for fashion, cologne, or some other consumer product. But these promotional elements are all a function of the broader promotional mix of marketing of which advertising is only one part. It is likely that today expenditures on other aspects of marketing, such as sales promotion, are greater than those on traditional forms of advertising. This is not merely a semantic difference, between sales promotion and advertising, as advertising is only one part of the larger marketing process; only one element in the mix. Furthermore, the marketing process is a part of the capitalistic economy in which we live. Once advertising is placed within the context of marketing, and once the marketing function is placed within the context of a capitalist economy, as Rotzell, Haefner, and Sandage (1976) point out, we begin to understand the rules of the game. The complexity of advertising's role within the financial economy is matched by its complex role in the cultural economy. It requires a multidimensional approach to understand advertising's place and purpose and to do so, this examination of advertising in everyday life will extend beyond its role in the financial economy. Bogart (1995) suggested advertising's economic function is misleading. There is a need to jettison the economic function of advertising from the social and cultural function if we are going to make generalizations about advertising's cultural role.

This book's primary focus is on the integration of national consumer goods advertising into everyday American life. And although it constitutes approximately 13% of all advertising, national consumer goods advertising is different from most local or regional retail advertising. National consumer goods advertising is the advertising one thinks of when one generally thinks of advertising: 30-second network television commercials or full-page national magazine advertisements. Such advertising is different in content and nature than sales promotions and retail advertising, which are more direct in their appeal and approach; the selling message is more obscure. It tends to rely heavily on image and atmospherics. Fowles (1996) referred to this as *compound* advertising. "The task of the advertisement is to get consumers to transfer the positive associations of the noncommodity material into the commodity, so that freedom and ruggedness equal Marlboro cigarettes, and friendship equals Bud Light" (11). The goal of much national consumer goods advertising is not the direct sale, but brand awareness or some other step on the hierarchy of effects. The hierarchy of effects—awareness, knowledge, liking, preference, conviction, and purchase—suggests that the goal of advertising is not always purchase and that stages of communication have to be accomplished before purchase is achieved.[2] Other theories suggest, however, that individuals can make purchases based on the emotional appeal of a product without knowing very much about it. And by the same token, it is possible to make a purchase decision based on knowledge, without any feeling toward the product or service. Such models as "Learn, Feel, Do Circles" suggest that the road from awareness to purchase may not be as straight forward as the hierarchy of effects would lead one to believe. This "Learn, Feel, Do" model suggests that consumers can (do) purchase a product before they (learn) know much about it. Also, consumers can feel emotionally connected to a product (feel) without knowing much about it (learn).

Expenditures on advertising in 1980 reached $53 billion. In 2000, approximately $233 billion was spent annually on advertising (Belch & Belch, 2001).[3] Approximately 60% of those annual expenditures were for national consumer goods advertising. These figures do not include expenditures for associated sales promotions. And the industry employs more than 250,000 people. Such extraordinary expenditures suggest that advertising must be effective. However, this assumption is fraught with controversy. The controversy as to whether or not advertising works to directly sell products is not new as famed retailer John Wannamaker, once said that he knew that half his advertising worked, but did not know which half.[4] Admittedly, there is an awful lot of advertising today. Approximately 1,500 ads are marched in front of our eyes every day. Do corporations advertise so much because consumers do not remember or do not pay attention to much advertising? The problem is, no one really knows to what extent advertising contributes to the sale of products. The preoccupation with the cause-and-effect relationship throws us off the scent of experiences and uses of advertising in everyday life.

Clearly, it is possible for an advertisement or perhaps a long-term campaign, for various but complex reasons, to be effective. By effective I mean it may temporarily lead to—for a period of time—an increase in sales of a product or it may merely mean heightened awareness of a new product being introduced to the market. But, within the construct of effectiveness little or nothing may happen. The latter possibility is confirmed by the fact that most new products introduced fail to penetrate the market. Beyond this range of possibilities, little else is known about the actual impact of advertisements on the financial economy. Perhaps the hierarchy of effects previously alluded to is based on a false premise, as advertisements do not operate in a vacuum. In other words, the creation of "awareness" is not under the sole control of the advertisers. The complexities of the marketing system, as well as social and cultural issues, need to be considered along with the individual consumer's role in this process. For example, Clairol hair coloring advertises its own hair coloring products as a part of a long-standing national consumer goods campaign. However, its advertisements also are a part of the total of advertisements for personal care products directed toward a particular target audience. The impact of such advertising, in this and other instances, goes beyond the product per se to lead us to speculate on its connection to and impact on other social issues like body image that is conveyed through, for example, ultra thin models depicted in personal care advertisements. In line with this thinking, critics have charged that fashion and cosmetic advertising is responsible, among other things, for the spread of anorexia and bulimia in our society. But the complex relationship that exists between advertising and its audiences makes it difficult to pinpoint what advertising's effects on society are, much less how effective an advertisement is in selling a product. John Wannamaker clearly understood advertising's limitations and in that the complexity of the marketplace when he proclaimed that much advertising fails.

ADVERTISING IN EVERYDAY LIFE

Perhaps there are other things at work beyond the advertiser's attempt to sell products; other ways in which consumers experience and use advertising in the context of their everyday lives. I am referring to experiences and uses that are not accounted for in the dominant paradigm regarding advertising's effectiveness. But the broader question remains: How do we experience advertising within the ordinary practices of everyday American life? In order to understand this, we need to consider the magical system of which advertising is a part (a subject discussed in chap. 2) and to look closely at language and behavior, what de Certeau (1984) referred to as *everyday practices*, that may extend beyond the arena of commerce to include other areas of every day social life. It is important to place advertising within the complexity of other contexts—cultural and social—in order to see how individuals "operate" within the culture.

In order to understand the work advertising does in the culture—and in that, the work we do with advertising—it is important to describe and interpret a range of uses to which individuals put advertising in the context of their everyday lives. As an example, during the 1996 Christmas shopping season, clothing designer Calvin Klein ran an advertising campaign for CK jeans the result of which brought a U.S. Justice Department investigation into child pornography. The highly imagistic advertisements placed, what at first glance appeared to be, very young models in rather seductive positions wearing, of course, CK jeans. After the investigation, the department quietly dropped its charges. This incident provides an opportunity to examine some of the work advertising does in U.S. culture and society and the work we do with it. Like Charles Dickens' *A Christmas Carol*, advertising in contemporary American society can be a moral tale. The CK jeans advertisements themselves along with different interest groups and individuals attracted to the advertisements played key cultural roles in this contemporary myth-making process and provide lessons about our society and ourselves.

These lessons are presented not only through the advertisements, but through the interactions of a strange group of bedfellows that include: The Calvin Klein Corporation and its namesake and chief spokesperson Calvin Klein, the U.S. Justice Department, media outlets like MTV that ran the advertising and reported on it when it made news, and special interest groups like the American Family Association of Tupelo, Mississippi, headed by Rev. Donald Wildmon. The fallout from this campaign had little to do with those effects traditionally associated with advertising, namely the sale of goods and services. These groups and individuals, among others, are cultural negotiators who participate in the production of meanings and in that the social practice of advertising. Of course, from this perspective what is learned has little to do with the products being sold as advertising takes on a broader cultural role.

In the course of this controversy, Calvin Klein was depicted in the mainstream media and trade press as a sinister business person operating at the fringe of acceptability, and simultaneously he was portrayed as a savvy business mogul for having generated free publicity way beyond that provided by the advertising time and space the corporation purchased. One trade journal reported positive responses that ranged from, "he got what he wanted" to "he spent half his ad budget and got double the publicity." As a result of this advertising campaign, Calvin Klein and his namesake corporation were depicted as immoral, but efficient capitalists. Historically, the immoral but successful business person has been associated with leading capitalists, including some of the greatest like John D. Rockefeller and Andrew Carnegie. Because capitalism has few moral guidelines governing how business should be conducted, part of our cultural understanding is that in order to be successful, sometimes you have to stretch or break the rules. This is reinforced through the public discourse generated by this campaign.

Public discourse regarding the Calvin Klein campaign grounds us in the rules of the game as it sets limits regarding what advertising can and cannot portray. That is where the U.S. Justice Department and the Rev. Donald Wildmon enter the picture. These external forces attempt to negotiate the social and legal limits, and Calvin Klein surely knew this as the corporation's advertising has in the past teetered on the edge of acceptability. The success of such a risky venture requires shrewd calculation. Is this a child pornographer, as some charged, or a capitalist doing good business? Or is the lesson that it takes one to achieve the other?

What about some of the others involved from whom these lessons are reinforced? MTV, for example, on whose channel the electronic versions of the advertisements ran, decided to drop the advertisements after public pressure mounted. Interestingly, all the advertisements had already aired by the time MTV agreed to take them off the air. Therefore, as a company whose primary business is selling advertising time, MTV emerged as a winner too. MTV can claim to have stopped running the ads (a moral decision) and claim they ran all the ads (a business decision).

Ironically, the vast majority of Americans probably never saw any of the advertisements from this campaign. And so it is mostly stakeholders that get caught up in the momentum using the opportunity to convey a moral understanding and use the advertisement as a point of engagement. Furthermore, special interest groups like a local PTA might use the advertisements in order to raise community awareness about child pornography or some related issue like child abuse. Clergy might use the advertisements as a point of discussion regarding what is right or wrong in society. And a group of teens might sit around talking about how "cool" the models in the advertisements look. The range of use here is very wide and provides evidence of how people can subvert the intention of the advertiser and find meanings that are relevant to their own lives. This example tells very little about the advertising campaign's effectiveness in moving product off the shelf. That, of course, is advertising's expressed intention. But we see by this example advertising is much more than that. Some variation of this scenario is repeated many times every day, perhaps not with the intensity of this advertising campaign. For example, Gillespie (1995) tracked how British teenagers in the course of their everyday lives used "ad talk" to negotiate their identities. She said, "One of the most tangible examples of the way that the discourses of TV and everyday life are intermeshed is when jingles, catch-phrases and humorous storylines of favorite ads are incorporated into everyday speech. Ads provide a set of shared cultural reference points, images and metaphors which spice local speech" (178). The contemporary world of advertising abounds with opportunities to understand ourselves and the world around us.

As advertising sometimes becomes fodder for social discourse, it periodically impacts language as a slogan, catch phrase, or jingle finds its way into everyday speech. For example, Wendy's fast food restaurants claimed a brief increase in sales when in 1984 the catch phrase "Where's the Beef?" pervaded U.S. society. The catch phrase lives on today as it was jettisoned from the Wendy's campaign and became ingrained in everyday U.S. language. As Americans, we speak in terms of "go power" and "where the rubber meets the road" and declare that if "Mikey will eat anything," perhaps so can we. Advertising's language may extend beyond its initial function to serve, for example, as expedient communication, a necessity in fast-paced American society. Such social uses of advertising language are examples of what de Certeau described as "poetic ways of making do," and extend our understanding of the ways advertising circulates within the discourse of everyday life. Advertising language is strategic and to a great extent automatic in the ways in which an individual sometimes injects conversations with the lively patter of slogans and catch phrases. As an expression of everyday speech, the use of catch phrases and slogans speaks to the postmaterialist culture in which we live and the ways we experience advertising in everyday life. To this end, advertising makes a small contribution to culture and society; it gives us something to talk about, something to think about and something to dream about. The particularities of advertising language show up in their everyday speech, and as a part of the individual's imaginary social world where advertising or elements thereof are incorporated into our internal dialogue. In addition to the pleasure it may bring, advertising provides social utility and contributes to social identity.

ADVERTISING AND THE AUDIENCE

The question of attention is one that is central to understanding advertising's broader work in the culture. The adage that the business of the commercial media is to deliver an audience to an advertiser is based on the understanding that people will pay attention to media. The commercial media system—newspapers, TV, magazines, the Internet, and so on—essentially rents out the attention of audiences to advertisers. Behaviorally, the audience is conceptualized as sitting stoically in front of the television or magazine for extended periods of time absorbing its content. If a viewer is paying attention to a sitcom, drama, or news program, for example, he or she will also pay attention to the commercials, or so the theory suggests. However, viewing does not equal attention. Bogart (1995) said, "Readers, viewers, and listeners have a built-in capacity for selective inattention" (76). Even when eyes are fixed on the screen or page, individuals may not be paying attention to the content of advertisements. Even when they do pay attention to an advertisement, they may, through some visual or verbal cue within the advertisement, begin to daydream. Campbell (1987) described the importance of daydreaming to the consumption process. He referred to imaginative pleasure seeking as an essential activity of consumption, more essential than the purchase of products. Selective inattention is not a psychological state, but rather a social practice. Coupled with the controversial area of audience measurement and the realization that advertisers, and in that the media, really do not know who is watching, listening, or reading, the generally held goal of media to deliver an audience to an advertiser is fraught with problems (Ang, 1991).

The notion that advertisers attempt to gain consumers' attention and keep it in order to communicate a message only considers the advertiser's desire, but does not consider the consumer's experience. The assumption is that individuals spend much of their free time watching television (the TV is on in the average home for approximately 7 hours a day), and additional time with other commercial media. In practice, individuals may not pay close attention to advertising or the programming for that matter even when their eyes are focused on the screen or page. In this age of the Internet, people multitask, that is they may surf the Net while listening to music or they may semi-watch television. No matter how sophisticated the methodology used by ratings services to track viewing or magazine reading, they cannot know what is going on in the individual's mind while he or she is consuming commercial media.

Attention is one of those illusory attributes that are complicated by one of advertising's major enemies—the remote control. The remote is a device that allows viewers to switch away from, rather than watch, commercials. Ang (1991) described zipping and zapping as "a cultural battle being acted out" (75). She added, "All in all, advertisers are clearly increasingly worried about the fact that viewers can actively avoid watching the commercials that are embedded in the programs" (76). However, in addition to the actual zapping with a remote control device, viewers can mentally tune out commercials, metaphorically changing stations in their own minds—a form of mental zapping. The remote control device allows the viewer to surf the spectrum of channels or switch between programs and/or commercials. As a result of all this literal channel surfing and the metaphoric form, the question of attention to advertising becomes more complex if not confounded.

In their effort to arrest viewers' attention, advertisers may employ strategies gleaned from entertainment that require the advertisement's message to extend far beyond the product's attributes. One industry approach to the audience problem is to make advertising so entertaining that consumers will feel compelled to watch, read, or listen to it. The result, however, is less than satisfactory as bits and pieces of advertisements sometimes serve as cues that cause viewers to begin daydreaming about things other than the product being advertised. As a result, viewers, listeners, or readers in some cases will remember parts of an advertisement, or they may remember an advertisement, but disconnect elements of it from the product. Other times, consumers will "get it wrong" by misconstruing the name of the product. In addition to what is going on in the consumer's mind, we also understand that sometimes advertising content serves as a cue to talk to someone in the room, make a phone call, get something to eat, in other words to do something else while the commercials are running.

An approach to studying advertising in everyday life would consider the advertising text and the way that text is used or reintegrated into everyday experience. This approach sees advertising as the sight of a struggle in which individuals negotiate acceptance or rejection of commercial messages. Advertising operates within a matrix in which the advertising industry seeks conformity to its messages and in reaction individuals create tactics to adapt it to their own rules. The terrain in which advertising operates is more like a moving equilibrium that has to be negotiated between the parties concerned.[5]

ADVERTISING AS SOCIAL PRACTICE

Media consumption—watching TV, listening to the radio, reading magazines, and surfing the Internet—is an integral part of everyday life and as such it is not a one-dimensional activity. There are different rituals in which individuals engage when they consume commercial media. Consumption itself is the manifestation of the ways in which we use advertising and through which we routinely attempt to subvert the intended meanings provided by advertisers. There are innumerable possibilities within the consumption process that allow for different kinds of viewers who may have different responses to the same advertisement based on their own interest. Through their consumption of advertising texts, individuals employ methods of transformation they may have honed over time.

Advertising as a social practice refers to the routine behaviors through which individuals consume advertising and it accounts for the tactics they use to make sense of their experience. Advertising sometimes becomes a point of confrontation and perhaps a struggle in which individuals develop tactics to deal with the strategically created messages. The "tactics of consumption" as de Certeau (1984) referred to them, encompass the "ingenious ways" to deal with the political dimension of everyday life. These tactics manifest in our interaction with others and how we process that advertising content within ourselves. Social practice also refers to what we do with advertising content away from media consumption; how we utilize it in our daily lives. This includes, but is not limited to, the way the elements of advertising enter into daily conversations, the ways in which advertising works in our daydreams and other stream of consciousness activity, as well as the ways in which it inhabits our dream world. Social practice also refers to the ways in which advertising encourages and enters into other aspects of our imagination, like the development of imaginary relationships with media figures.

Media consumption, like other everyday practices, as de Certeau suggested, is tactical. There is a political dimension to consuming advertising that is produced for the consumer. In this sense de Certeau (1984) referred to consumers as "textual poachers" (xi). *Textual poaching* is a social practice in which the individual appropriates meaning from a text, like advertising, that is intended to persuade. For de Certeau, appropriating an advertisement would be like renting an apartment. The apartment belongs to someone else, but the renter will re-arrange the furniture in order to make the dwelling their own. It is through such rituals of resistance that individuals make their own meanings through and with advertising. The rituals associated with the social practice of advertising are ways of making sense of the world in which we live. Granted, advertising is only one aspect of this social practice of consumption, but it is an important one.

The advertisement is the site of a struggle—a wholly unequal one—between producers who employ strategies to overcome resistance and consumers who apply tactics to resist. Whereas de Certeau (1984) placed much power on the part of individuals to resist the power of producers, Gramsci (1998) described a compromise equilibrium in which neither side necessarily "wins." On the micro-level, looking at the results of advertising as "compromise equilibrium" based on the political struggle for power at first glance appears to demonstrate how individuals appropriate the contents of advertisements for their own use in ways that are not envisioned by their producers.[6] Therefore, the question is not just about what advertising does to us. The question must also consider what we do to advertising. Within this line of thinking, it is important to understand the many ways in which individuals make culture through their experience of, with, and through advertising.[7] It is unclear whether it is advertising alone that makes this struggle possible, but we are engaged in an active relationship with it through which we find meaning, pleasure, and identity (Fiske, 1987).

> The power of consumers derives from the fact that meanings do not circulate in the cultural economy in the same way that wealth does in the financial. They are harder to possess (and thus to exclude others from possessing), they are harder to control because the production of meaning and pleasure is not the same as the production of the cultural commodity, or of other goods, for in the cultural economy the role of consumer does not exist as the end point of a linear economic transaction. Meanings and pleasures circulate within it without any real distinction between producers and consumers. (313)

In this sense, the social practice associated with the consumption of advertising is not something that can be imposed on people, rather it is something that people learn, through enculturation, to cope with, resist, and evade.

Other theorists have problems with the concept of resistance, at least the way in which Fiske may over-estimate it (Ang, 1996). The process of creating meaning and identity through the appropriation of advertising is not the work of an empowered audience, but rather "part and parcel of the chaotic system of capitalist postmodernity itself. In this sense, it would be mistaken to see the acting out of difference unambiguously as an act of resistance; what needs to be emphasized, rather, is that the desire to be different can be simultaneously complicit with and defiant against the institutionalization of excess of desire in capitalist modernity" (Ang, 1996: 179). Ang related this position back to de Certeau who described social practices as "escaping without leaving." Morris (1992) viewed the issue of resistance as a systemic one. For Morris, the celebration of resistance is a myth that is apparent only when one focuses on the micro aspects of media consumption when we take the evasive acts at face value. She rooted the notion of resistance in institutional issues of uncertainty, ambiguity, and the chaos that is built into the system. It is the "celebration of limitless flux (that serves) as a mechanism within its ordering principle" (Ang, 1991: 179). It may be that both theoretical approaches hold value for understanding advertising in everyday life as resistance in some form or other does exist at the micro-level and uncertainty and ambiguity at the macro-level. It is most likely that uncertainty (discussed in chap. 2) and ambiguity drive the individual into the system as consumers seek stability through the appropriation of advertising content, and it also may be true that within that institutional process individuals corrupt the message as they seek meaning, pleasure, and identity. Silverstone (1994) added that rather than looking at both (advertiser) strategies and (consumer) tactics, which he claimed are "unequally opposed" forces, the focus should be on "the expressions of activity and creativity within, and constitutive of, the mobile forces of structure" (164). The tension between "security and anxiety" that exist between advertiser and consumer can be studied through ethnographic research that accepts the structural relationships between the two as "transitional."

If the study of advertising is to be situated in the taken-for-grantedness of routine existence, then it is important to extend the ideas of those concerned primarily with media consumption to focus on the dynamic forces at work between advertiser and consumer, and among individuals and within individuals in the context of their everyday lives.

CONCLUSION

Advertising began as news.[8] Advertising evolved into information. It then became entertainment. Throughout U.S. history, advertising has come under attack. This is especially so when we reflect back on the past century to view the vital role advertising played in the development of an emerging consumer economy that saw advertising as a means to dispose of excess production. Today, advertising continues to serve all three of its original functions, but advertising as experience is one that has not been accounted for until recently. An advertisement whose central message and selling point are obscure, what I have referred to as national consumer goods advertising, may not be terribly relevant to consumers, but the associative meanings in the advertisements may give way to, in the postmodern sense, experience. The kind of experience to which I refer is a social practice through which individuals negotiate their way through advertising which in our contemporary society is difficult to escape.

Fiske (1987) argued that culture circulates in two economies, one financial and the other cultural. The financial economy is concerned in the case of advertising with the sale of products. In this chapter, I have posited that it is very difficult to find a causal link between advertising and the sale of goods and services. On the other hand, the cultural economy, of which advertising is a part, is concerned with "appropriation and use—meanings, pleasures and social identities" (Fiske, 1987: 311). The cultural economy is exemplified in the extended uses of electronic media, like video games and computers in which individuals can have an interactive experience with a television screen. Terkel (1995) wrote extensively about the immersion into multi-user domains (MUDs) via computer-generated fantasies. As such interactive video games and the Internet have become the model for more sophisticated experience with media content. Like the experience in MUDs, the notion that one can experience an advertisement transcends the way in which we have traditionally viewed media consumption.

We may not be able to determine the answer to the question: Does advertising work? Twitchell (1996) maintained that advertising is more like window dressing whose primary purpose is to make corporations feel good. However, more can be known about the work advertising does in the culture and the work we do with advertising. In order to do so, the consumer has to be conceptualized in a way that conceives of audiences as producers and consumers of meanings. It is imperative under such a framework to consider the text of advertising within particular social contexts. In this way, the reader will see where advertising "lives" and how Americans experience advertising as a part of their everyday lives.

ENDNOTES

1. For a discussion of how advertisements like those for Benetton and Calvin Klein "work" see Meyers (1999).
2. The hierarchy of effects theory is attributed to Lavidge and Steiner who developed it in 1961.
3. Learn, Feel, Do Circles are one model of how the hierarchy of effects works.
4. This famed remark has also been link to Lord Levermore, founder of Lever Brothers.
5. Moving equilibrium suggests that the advertising system is inherently unstable and can be complicated by both internal and external factors.
6. Gramsci's compromise equilibrium implies a fixed point. However, near equilibrium and far from equilibrium need to be accounted for within the varying states of equilibrium.
7. By experience of, with and through advertising, I refer to our reactions to advertisements, the incorporation of its content within our inner dialogue, and the social discourse through which we use the language of advertising.
8. Among other functions, early newspapers served as a responsible report of commercial transactions, and this news was an important part of everyday life. During the Middle Ages, "country men and gentry traveled to fairs to swap the news" (Emery, 1972: 3).

2

THE CARNIVALESQUE, ADVERTISING MAGIC AND THE GAMES WE PLAY

Included among the strategies utilized by advertisers is an ever-evolving grab bag of creative "magic tricks" available as enticements to consumers. This slight of hand, a simple deception in the guise of entertainment, is intended to encourage consumers to engage with the advertisement and enter its fictive world. By enticements I do not mean the explicit offer that may be part of the message, like specific features and benefits of a product or service. Here, I refer to the structural tricks within advertisements and the use of media figures and other techniques to entice consumers to engage with the advertisement. This dialectic between advertiser strategies and consumer tactics is like a cat and mouse game. Additionally, beyond the creative devices used in specific advertisements, on the macro-level magic is built into the system of commerce. By that I mean during the process of engagement with consumers when advertising attempts to sell products and services, it also attempts to sell us ourselves, but not just our ordinary selves (Williamson, 1991). Williamson claimed that some of the time advertising is so compelling as to provide a short-lived vicarious experience through the presentation of an idealized vision of everyday life, one that may temporarily lift us out of our mundane existence. Or as Silvertsone (1994) put it, "goods are imagined before they are purchased" (26).

This chapter considers advertising's basis in the world of magic and wonder. I suggest that wonder, which advertising sometimes evokes, is closely tied to an individual's consent to participate with its content and perhaps to use its content in the multiple discourse strategies of everyday life. The chapter discusses advertising as a replacement for the loss of tactility experienced due to our distancing from the process of production and the invocation of imagination as a substitute. The ways in which advertising seeks both to stabilize and destabilize the marketplace are described along with its relationship to the meaning making system that is the end product of our experience with the magical qualities of advertising.

THE FICTIVE WORLD OF ADVERTISING

The idealized vision of an American way of life presented by advertisers comes up against its relative significance for the individual consumer who may under certain circumstances be willing to participate in the dialectic that the advertising "text" promotes as a function of the multiple discourses of everyday life. In many ways, advertising's idealized vision is perhaps the least "open" text delivered by the mass media. Perhaps that is why advertisements utilize myriad "tricks" to encourage individuals to engage with it and enter into its fictive world. By least open text I mean that advertising, unlike entertainment or news, has a specific message it must convey. Entertainment, for example, is presented in a way that allows for different members of an audience to interpret the content within their own belief system. That is what S. Hall (1980) meant by reading with, against, or taking a negotiated position toward a text. With regard to entertainment, producers and editors do not mind this variation within the "readings" of the text. Advertisers, however, would prefer that consumers not read against or negotiate their texts. To that end, advertising is crafted as a closed or semi-closed text in which the consumer is led in a specific direction.

Advertisements are highly crafted sales messages that generally are targeted to specific demographic or psychographic groups. The messages and images are crafted in a way to appeal specifically to individuals in those groups. This narrow casting of the advertiser's net, also referred to as target marketing, gets (from the advertiser's point of view) the correct message in the proper medium, within the appropriate media environment, directed to a very specific audience. In this sense, advertisers cannot allow for the dominant idealized vision that may be conveyed in the background to be foregrounded by material that leads to multiple interpretations. Allowing for multiple interpretations would be economically inefficient. When advertisers set an objective for their campaign to create knowledge about the product or liking for the product (two steps on the advertising hierarchy of effects), the advertisement is crafted to obtain measurable results. The latitude for openness within the text of the advertisement is severely limited for this reason. Raymond Williams' (1980) classic essay, "Advertising: The Magic System" described advertising as being like the mythical Pied Piper in which unknowing consumers blindly follow the piper's lead. The closed-text approach just described is consistent with Williams' contention that consumers are cultural dupes.

However, in practice advertisements rarely work this way. The consumer's role needs to be accounted for in this process. Consider for example the idea of "newness" built into our belief system of "planned obsolescence" that may encourage some consumers under some circumstances to imagine themselves in a new automobile. But just as likely, others may "read against" an advertisement for an automobile that they cannot afford or do not need. Within the range of reactions toward an advertisement, an individual may imagine him or herself driving down the street in a brand new automobile seen in an advertisement and still decide not to purchase it. There are other points on the continuum of meaning or what Storey (1999), Grossberg (1997), and Radway (1998) called nomadic subjectivity—the ability to produce a range of meanings from the dominant or preferred meaning to oppositional meanings.

There are social dimensions to this meaning-making system where consumers socially situate themselves by discussing, for example, the advertisements that appeared during the Super Bowl or some other national event. Such water cooler talk is not accounted for in the vision of the way advertising is supposed to work as presented here. With regard to the Super Bowl, water cooler talk is part of a ritual practice in which individuals occasionally participate, however, such talk does not consider the direct transfer of information from the advertisement to the individual. This practice requires other individuals to participate in the meaning-making system, and perhaps as an ancillary outcome, to spread awareness of a product or service. This is hardly a reliable system that advertisers can count on. This is particularly so because advertisers simply do not know which advertisements consumers are going to talk about and what they are going to say when they do talk about advertisements. Advertising becomes part of the cultural repertoire of resources available to the individual to use as part of their discursive strategy. It is this type of experience that, simply put, makes life more enjoyable and fosters the imagination.

It is important to acknowledge that in the course of their everyday routines, individuals selectively participate and may choose not to participate with the content of advertising as it clutters their media experience and overloads them with non-relevant material. The degree to which individuals express their willingness to participate in the fictive world of advertising is indicative of advertising's magical qualities and the work that it does in the culture and society. This point of confrontation and perhaps struggle between advertising's compelling messages and the individual's consent to participate with and through advertising is expressed through an individual's discourse strategy. The concept of coercion with regard to advertising gives way to the attempt to manufacture consent or at least the acquiescence toward it. Advertising is, therefore, uniquely rooted in the world of magic and wonder and sometimes individuals selectively participate.

ADVERTISING AND MAGIC

Through advertising's magical qualities products, images and related social scenes and situations are fed back to consumers as misrepresentation: Advertising is out of place and out of time. Magic in advertising, Williamson (1991) said, is a "mythical means of doing things" (140).

> Magic always involves the misrepresentation of time in space, or space in time. Time is magically incorporated into space, in such things as the crystal ball—an object which contains the future—and space is magically produced out of time, in conjuring up objects out of nowhere, instantly, by means of spells or alchemy. In the center of these magical processes, the axis of their performance, is the subject: you, the buyer or user of the product. (140)

Twitchell (1996) confirms that advertising's magical quality continues today, adding that advertising's content is full of magical characters. Williamson (1991) claimed advertising's magical quality creates a never-ending exchange between passivity and action. Within Williamson's perspective, advertising is compensation for inactivity. *Inactivity* is, of course, another term for the contemporary term *couch potato*, but no less pejorative in its incantation of nonrational consumer behavior. Advertising's content has the potential to be magical; that is to say, it may figuratively, for a period of time, take viewers, readers, and listeners out of the ordinary and into the extraordinary. To suggest that the result of that magic is automatically a passive consumer is to miss the forest for the trees. Jhally (1989) said that as consumers become accustomed to magical claims presented in advertisements, those claims become plausible. However, there is little evidence in the daily practices of consumers to support this position. Rather, Jhally and Williamson, among others, draw their conclusions from analysis of the advertisements themselves, not by investigating the social practices associated with the consumption of advertising. The question really is not about passive or active consumers of advertising, but rather about the degree of significance (Storey, 1999).

ADVERTISING AND TACTILE EXPERIENCE

Our understanding of the magical qualities and the variability of consumer response to advertising is rooted in the history of commerce. Advertising historian Jackson Lears (1994) pointed out that for centuries (1500–1800) commerce was connected to a carnival atmosphere, the fantastic and the magical. During this early modern period there was a merger of the religious carnival and the market fair. "The market fair brought locally rooted townsfolk and peasants into contact with the exotic and the bizarre: with magicians and midgets, quacks and alchemists, transient musicians and acrobats; peddlers of soap from Turkey, needles from Spain, and looking-glasses from Venice" (Lears, 1994: 24).

The carnival of the marketplace, a social experience centering on raw materials and crafts, over time was displaced as individuals became physically and socially distanced from the production process. As the marketplace changed along with the emergence of mass media so did the social arrangement of purchasing behaviors change with the end product being an increase in the importance of advertising's magical qualities. The changes in the marketplace go beyond the mere exchange of information to denote changes in the relationship between the consumer and the marketplace and a change in the relationship between the consumer and material goods.

Over the past two centuries in America, the marketplace changed to become more professional—more detached—and as a result added a layer of disconnection from the raw materials of production. "Marx argued that under capitalist conditions of production and distribution, products of labor appear as abstract things detached from the labor process. They are offered for sale in markets separate from the place of production. All kinds of special attributes are imputed to these commodities" (Gottdiener, 2000: 4). Under these conditions, consumption becomes less of a tactile practice associated with production and moves toward a consumer society based more on creating a symbolic connection between goods and services and fulfilling consumer wants as opposed to their needs. It was this disembodiment of abundance imagery, according to Lears, that led to the model of organizational life that is centered on the abstract notion of "keeping up with the Jones." The point here is that products became abstracted from their raw form and craft associated with production and were transformed by manufacturing, distribution, and communication within a new aesthetic. For example, in the latter part of the 19th century, before branding of products became the norm, one could go to a general merchandise store and reach into the cracker barrel and scoop up a pound or so of generic crackers. The consumer could see the product, touch it and taste it, and purchase however much she or he wanted, but there were no brands from which to choose.

Lears (1994) said, "It wasn't until the early twentieth century that the rise of corporate advertising brought a disembodiment of abundance imagery, as the carnivalesque celebration of fleshly excess was streamlined into an exaltation of industrial efficiency, and the process of productivity became a model for the organization of everyday life" (19). Accordingly, advertising has its roots in commerce and the marketplace and therefore it too is rooted in the fantastic and magical. Early 20th century advertising included much product information as new technologies brought forth to the marketplace many new mass-produced products. As these new products—radios, refrigerators, and automobiles—became available and perhaps commonplace, fewer new products entered the market. Marked by increased competition, advertising in the 1920s was generally informative, at least by today's standards. The predominant style of advertising copy at that time was referred to as "reason why" (Fox, 1984). The advertising was imagistic although by today's standards the images lacked sophistication. The objective of the advertising based on sound psychological reasoning was to appeal to rational decision making to give the consumer a reason to use the product.[1]

Advertising is the manifestation of this disembodiment, as it depicts a hyper-reality that becomes the idealized vision of everyday life that consumers may choose to engage with based on their own discursive strategy. One of the most consistent attributes of advertising is its ability to invoke the carnival atmosphere and take the viewer, reader, or listener beyond the ordinary. As Jason Rogers, the publisher of the *New York Globe* said in 1919, advertising is "something alien and foreign, a magic force" (cited in Bogart, 1995: 127). To a great extent, an audience's willingness to suspend disbelief, to engage in fantasy activity, and to enter into the imaginary world of goods and services—including the places and people who inhabit them—is an important factor in understanding the cultural experience of advertising.

Advertising, once considered akin to "mere slight of hand, or a diffuse sense of the marvelous erupting amid the everyday," was adapted for 20th century use and systematized by marketers in order to provide steady fuel for the "engines of economic development" (Lears, 1994: 19-20). From the marketer's point of view, advertising could be utilized to create order out of a naturally volatile market. It is ironic that something as uncontrollable as the advertising message is seen as the source of economic stability. Furthermore, this suggests that magic is the chosen "tool" of producers wishing to stabilize the marketplace.

In contemporary society, as the practice of consumption becomes abstracted from actual experience, advertising's magical transformation of the marketplace grows in importance. The concepts of *magic* and *carnival* have always been associated with the market-place, but they have been transformed in contemporary society to become part of a cultural practice and the way consumers experience advertising in everyday life. Advertising's symbolic expressions and transformative powers are precisely what critics have used to attack advertising as the permissible lie, hyperbole, manipulative, and persuasive, in other words, magic. A simplified example of the transformational powers of postmodern marketing can be seen in the ways consumers interact with their televisions via the Home Shopping Network and other like services. There is no tactile experience associated with the purchase and the only actual interaction is via the telephone as the consumer completes the transaction not with hard currency, but with a credit card. Similarly the Internet offers a simulated shopping experience where one cannot touch the goods and pays for purchases electronically. It is this very distancing that promotes and encourages participation in the magical world of advertising.

To a greater extent today we are literally and figuratively distanced from the raw materials and the goods themselves; in a sense we are protected from them and them from us. Purity, sterility, and hygiene are the hallmarks of products we consume. This goes beyond food to encompass other "hard" goods as well. Consider, for example, the packaging of the home computer: surrounded in Styrofoam and bagged in plastic and secured in a cardboard box. At a supermarket you cannot hold crackers in your hand, rather you can only hold a box of crackers and compare them perhaps to another box. This absence of tactility can be seen through the experience of a child riding in his or her parent's shopping cart up and down the aisles of a supermarket. Children marvel with wonderment and amazement at the myriad products. And when they get to the cereal aisle, one with particular appeal to them, their excitement grows ever more apparent. But what are they marveling at? The cereal cannot be viewed, cannot be tasted. The modern supermarket is like a postmodern carnival of sorts as there is so much from which to choose and by which to be entertained. It is a microcosm of a fair where merchants hawk their goods. But the sales pitch has become transparent and the goods sanitized as the institution of marketing transformed the purchasing process.

Today, we choose containers and colors along with images that align or associate products with values consistent with our own. The loss of tactility makes advertising an ever more important facet of the system of commerce. Advertising serves as a replacement for the tactile response to consumer goods as we use the symbolism offered by advertising to achieve a synthetic form of authenticity. Advertising is a postmodern form of magic through which wonder intensifies experience, even though the experience lacks authenticity.

AUDIENCES AND UNCERTAINTY

Fortini-Campbell points out that for the marketer of goods and services change has become a way of life in contemporary American society. She furthermore submits that "changes now taking place in the world of marketing are so fundamental and irreversible that they force us to set aside our old assumptions" (6). Markets are not stable and neither are companies or their employees. Technology is changing at a rapid rate. Consumer taste is fickle; brand loyalty a thing of the past. In this book, I am primarily concerned with instability as it relates to audiences of advertising. I do not mean to suggest that consumers are unstable in some psychological manner. However, beyond merely being fickle about brand loyalty, marketers of goods and services are unable to control consumers through advertising. What we now know about audiences is that they are "individual, social and cultural entities" (Silverstone, 1994: 132). Silverstone pointed out:

> Audiences too have varying degrees of freedom to construct a rela-
> tionship to the individual texts of the medium or to the medium as a
> whole. Individuals can be deeply moved (for better and worse) by
> what they see and hear on the screen. Others can, and do, ignore
> those images and sounds, or let them slip away like water in the
> sand. For yet others, as I have argued, the continuities of soap
> operas or of television itself offer a kind of security otherwise
> unavailable through other media. And even more, there is the drip
> feed of the longue duree, the more or less consistent, more or less
> resistant, diet of ideology and entrenched values, invisibly informing
> and constraining all kinds of social action and belief. (133)

Although, as Silverstone pointed out, individuals vary in their degree of connectedness to advertisements, the industry attempts to constrain audiences through the multiplicity of ways they attempt to make determinations about them. In other words, advertisers attempt to unify individuality through constraining techniques like demographics, psychographics, and geodemographics, among others. But these means of constraining audiences do not account for the multiple ways in which individuals use advertising in their everyday lives.

Contradictory forces are at work here—stability and instability. Advertisers desperately want to stabilize the marketplace and they do so by de-centering the individual consumer. Ang (1996) said, "What is historically particular about capitalist postmodernity's 'true realm of uncertainty' has to do with the system's ambiguous stance toward the infinitude of the social itself: as much as it wants to control it, it also depends on exploiting it" (176). Ang suggested that planned obsolescence, as exemplified by the ever-changing fashion system, feeds into the "idea that constant transformation of identities (through consumption) is pleasurable and meaningful" (177).

Advertisers attempt to control audiences through the magical qualities they deploy encouraging consumers through magical enticements or by blatantly chasing after them. The view that magic—advertising—is a means to stabilize an uncertain marketplace, that is, the flow of goods from producer to consumer, may have been consumption capitalism's most pervasive vision, but there is something more in this magic for those who attend the carnival. For example, in its attempt to control the socially produced wants of consumers, the advertising industry utilizes signifiers, like celebrities, to ground their products in a symbolic association between the two. As celebrities appear on the screen or page they are presented as "empty" or "flat" one-dimensional characters as Lears (1994), Schudson (1984), and Gitlin (1993) suggested. However, when an individual confronts those flattened images in an advertisement she or he may selectively inflate them and imbue them with meaning in ways that may not be fully comprehended by advertisers.

As marketers seek to control uncertainty as with, for example, the deployment of celebrities in advertisements, consumers sometimes attempt to evade them in the ways individuals reintegrate aspects of those celebrities into their everyday lives; a cat and mouse game ensues. This points up that the magic of advertising requires individuals within an audience for whom the content is significant enough so that they are willing to participate through consent and wonder. But the magic may or may not work the way the advertiser hopes, as in the case of celebrities who appear in advertisements.[2]

The consumer's ability to use advertising information in order to make a product selection is coupled with and processed through the advertisement's symbolic alignment with social, cultural, psychological, and economic values that individuals bring to the decision-making process. Advertising, of course, plays a part in this transformational process, but not necessarily as the sole source of information on which to make a decision. It must be stressed that transformation is not a straightforward (controllable) process. The proof of this can be found in the exceedingly few new products that successfully enter the marketplace and the decreasing number of competitive products. Therefore, advertisers expend huge sums of money in order to give greater meaning to products that already exist. As it has moved through the product life cycle, one would quickly run out of fingers counting the times that Tide laundry detergent, for example, has been declared "new and improved" by Proctor and Gamble. But "new and improved" only root Tide in its own history and in this history "new and improved" seemingly lends stability to the advertising process. Information about brightening or cleaning agents is secondary to the connections to modern life that the advertisements provide. In essence, the ingredients of the product may change, however, American home life as envisioned by advertisers remains traditional or at least squarely within the norms of present day society.[3] Additionally, advertising sometimes transcends the product's attributes in an effort to connect to other forms of relevance, other things the advertiser thinks the consumer will find meaningful.

In an attempt to create and maintain stability, advertisers fill a cultural void by replacing the tactile experience of the marketplace transaction. The importance of this shift cannot be overstated: As production and consumption changed for the individual from a tactile experience to a cognitive activity, advertising changed from a cognitive process to a tactile one. We do not just view advertising from a distance looking only for information on which to make rational decisions, now, we may experience advertising's organic quality. It is advertising's magical quality that makes this experience possible, opening up the possibility to engage with the contents of advertisements and perhaps to reintegrate them into our everyday lives.

As transformation of the marketplace continues, advertising's social and cultural role remains vital. In essence, the more distanced we are from the source, the greater advertising's role in providing the social and culture "glue" that binds us to a market economy, thus reducing uncertainty in the marketplace. The social distancing from the actual marketplace can be seen clearly through the advent of the ATM or automatic teller at the local bank. Tele-banking and computerized banking over the Internet further distances the consumer from the physical presence of the bank and bank personnel (e.g., actual transactions). Presently, one can transact banking matters without ever having direct contact with another human being. There is no actual social interaction connected to the ATM or Internet banking services, and as a result this consumer activity has become quite sterile.[4] Advertising, therefore, takes on a newer broader role providing the foundations for a social connection between consumer and producer to stabilize the relationship by inflating the advertising experience with meaning. The nature of that connection may vary from product to product and the social roles—outward directed authority figure or friend—extending beyond the traditional ones to encompass a simulated or artificial social experience. This role goes beyond the information provided by advertisements and their depictions of efficient modern life.

The simulated connections that advertising provides may transcend its traditional social role, as the pervasiveness of advertising is something Americans have come to accept. Advertising as experience supplants other experiences traditionally associated with consumer transactions. To some degree, advertising has replaced or supplanted other social interaction between producer and consumer. Therefore, our understanding of the cause-and-effect relationship must be expanded to include connections that extend beyond product and purchase. The desire for stability in the marketplace supplements the advertiser's desire to control the social world through the presentation of idealized visions of everyday life, but the connections to the products advertised per se may be tangential. Consumers' willingness to participate is part of the magical experience of advertising.

MAKING, REMAKING, AND UNMAKING MEANING

The way individuals experience advertising has been described as being under a spell (Williamson, 1991). Advertising's magical qualities, Williamson said, are rooted in a kind of determinism in which the results are always fixed. She described the magical forces of determinism as "a sort of pre-scientific ordering of nature" within which there is some "inherent causality" (143). A fundamental problem with this meaning-effects approach to advertising is the suggestion that advertisements will necessarily produce a predictable outcome. As individuals participate in the magic of advertising, they engage in the transformational system that Williamson admitted is a "short cut," twisting the magical with actual experience (140). To the contrary, Eco (1980) described this "short cut" as aberrant decoding in which the significant social differences between producers and consumers of texts will necessarily produce aberrant readings. Similarly, Storey (1999) suggested that individuals make texts—advertisements—meaningful through "actual practices of cultural consumption" (157). Storey said:

> Texts may be characterized by "structured polysemy," organized to generate "preferred readings," to offer to readers specific positions of understanding and intelligibility, but what they cannot do is to guarantee that particular meanings or specific reading positions will be taken up. To know how a text is activated requires the study of actual audiences. (157)

Although advertising may beckon the individual into its magical world, as Storey suggested, a meaningful experience or "preferred reading" is not an automatic outcome when considering the range of possible experiences individuals may have with and through advertising. In their everyday lives, individuals do not necessarily find the intended meaning that may be located in a commercial message. Whether the concern is for the "preferred meanings" (S. Hall, 1980) of the dominant culture or the "oppositional meanings" (Fiske, 1989) of the subservient culture, meaning is central to those concerned with mass media content, and in that advertising as a social practice of lived cultures of everyday life. The traditional framework for understanding the ways in which individuals "read" an advertisement are bound by the belief that the message, whether one reads with or against it, is inherently meaningful. However, in order to understand its broader role in the symbolic system in which individuals operate in U.S. society, it is important to consider the possibility that advertising may not be perceived as meaningful, and perhaps misunderstood. Therefore, in addition to the dominant belief among critics and theorists that advertising creates meaning, we must consider that consumers remake or unmake meaning and allow for the potential for misunderstanding of advertising. It is also possible that consumers may, in a postmodern sense, substitute experience for meaning; in other words, they may appreciate the advertisement not for what it says, but for what it does on purely aesthetic levels.

There is a need to expand the way we conceptualize interpreted meaning in advertising and in that effectiveness or lack of meaning, including ambiguity. Miller posited that individuals are "very active, fluid and diverse" in the ways they "transform resources . . . into expressive environments, daily routines and often cosmological ideals" (8). Advertising may be viewed as a practice through which individuals sometimes make meaning when the content of an advertisement is attached to some context through which the individual attempts to make sense of their world or in which they attempt to find their place in the social order. Advertisers may use the wonder of magic to entice consumers in, but the various ways in which we make meaning, or do not, constitutes the game we play with it.

Storey (1999) said, "Advertising seeks to make a commodity an object of desire. But it also involves the work of desire and imagination engaged in by consumers prior to consumption, and of course informed but not controlled by the activities of advertisers" (165). Silverstone echoed this sentiment when he said, "the process of imagination is a dialectical one: driven by stimulation and desire, stalled by frustration and indifference, transformed by the active engagement of consumers in the very process of commodification" (126). He added, this transformative activity "opens up a space (*or not*) for imaginative and practical work on the meaning of the object" (126). It is important to keep in mind that meaning is rooted in the advertisement within its recognizable scenes, symbols, and other content, but not controlled by the text. However, it cannot be assumed that an advertising message is inherently meaningful, nor can it be assumed that an individual will find meaning in an advertisement. Appropriation takes place when individuals take the advertisement out of its media context and reintegrate it into their everyday lives. Through a complex interchange—the game—between the advertiser, the individual and a particular social context, some aspects of a commercial message may be rendered meaningful. Meaning in this sense gives way to experience through the act of appropriation. For example, there may be some aspects of the advertisement, like a celebrity spokesperson, through which individuals appropriate aspects of the celebrity's personality that may or may not be related to the advertisement, whereas the attributes of the product or other aspects of the advertisement's content are rendered ambiguous or meaningless. The way in which an individual might reintegrate some aspect of the celebrity into his or her own life represents the process of making common sense out of social experience. Considering the large amount of time in their daily lives that individuals spend with various media, including advertising, this process represents an active struggle to make sense out of their social experience.

Radway's (1991) seminal study of readers of romance novels is concerned with the interpretive strategies employed by readers of those novels. Similar to the way Radway's informants found meaning in romance novels, individuals may appropriate some aspect of advertising for use in a social context other than media consumption. The discursive strategies that individuals activate are connected to everyday routines—needs, desires, or intentions. Meaning is still Radway's central concern, but it is meaning that individuals find located in a social context. This contextual approach to appropriation leads to the understanding that meanings are in fact multiple. Fiske (1989) referred to those multiple meanings as polysemic. The task of the advertiser is to attempt to control meaning; in this sense advertising is a site of struggle in which "polysemy acts up the forces that oppose control" (Fiske, 1987: 93). Research has not yet fully answered the question regarding how many meanings exist: Are meanings like snowflakes, infinite? Rather, like advertising, meanings are culturally produced and are bound by the cultural experience of the individual. Perhaps as important is the question: How do we experience an advertisement in the routine of ordinary existence?

Lewis (1994) pointed out that ambiguity needs to be accounted for as a variation of experience. In other words, there is a range and variety of experiences that may (or may not) render advertisements meaningful, and within that range is ambiguity and perhaps vagueness. It is through this cultural framework that individuals experience, or perhaps do not experience, advertising. Twitchell (1996) described advertising as shallow because of its lack of depth and lack of historical context. Advertising, he said, is cultural junk. But it may be the very shallowness (inherent incompleteness) of advertising texts that allows for polysemy to do its work. In other words, advertising attempts to present a completed picture to the reader, viewer, or listener who may, or may not, embellish the canvas by imbuing it with meaning.

Beyond the inherent meaning in the text, the viewer, reader, or listener is called on to make sense of the advertisement. In the case of some advertisements, the symbols are universal as to allow for easy interpretation. Unlike a challenging novel, an advertisement that takes too much effort to interpret may cause consternation on the part of the consumer and perhaps render the advertisement worthless, at least from a marketing perspective. An individual might find an advertisement meaningless simply because the content is confusing.[5] Some advertisements rely so heavily on the imagistic and symbolic they don't make much sense. At other times, advertisers use puns in order to offer up two meanings, in this case they may make too much sense. In the former instance, this vagueness is created by intention in order to obscure the message as an attempt to lure in the consumer as she or he attempts to appropriate meaning. Through the meaninglessness of the message or ambiguity of the images, viewers or readers are left to their own devices where they can employ their own tactics of appropriation. A series of now classic advertisements that introduced the Infinity luxury cars, for example, never showed the automobile, but only elements of the earth (stone, rock, and water) exemplifying ambiguity in the content. The advertiser was attempting to create associations between these basic environmental elements and the automobile. However, such advertisements leave the viewer or reader much leeway with regard to interpretation. Such advertisements may be image rich, but inadvertently open up the text enough for broad interpretation. The vagueness of the content, perhaps, allows the recipients to "read into" the content, embellishing the canvas with their own devices. Or perhaps the superficiality of the advertisement, because there is little or ambiguous meaning in the advertisement's content, provides the viewer or reader with a limited opportunity to superficially experience the aesthetic images in the advertisement.

As consumers live within different referent systems, it is also possible to experience advertising content (meaningful content would include a recognizable structure, message, symbols and images) as meaningless. This outcome, based on its situational relevance or lack thereof, suggests that what might be relevant to one consumer, might not be relevant to another. Fiske (1989) rejected the term *consumer* and replaced it with *circulators of meaning*. One must ask: How can anyone circulate meaning when the content of the message obscures meaning or is devoid of meaning? For this very reason individuals may not "get" the point of an advertisement or they may misinterpret its message. Could it be that the meaning, like those advertisements for Infinity automobiles, is intentionally obscured rendering the message ambiguous? Ambiguity and vagueness are means by which the advertisement may be "opened up" for multiple interpretations and experience. This represents the struggle between the advertiser who wants to "close down" the interpretations or to open up the advertisement in a controlled manner, and a consumer who uses their own set of devices to appropriate or not appropriate meaning.

Advertising is like a staged magic show in which sometimes the audience simply does not get the trick. Through repeated exposure, individuals have become well practiced at seeing through and looking past much advertising. There are times when viewers, readers or listeners simply do not understand advertisements at all, particularly when the messages come at them in a series of 15- or 30-second snippets or when they are involved in other activities (multitasking) while consuming commercial media. It cannot be assumed that individuals are focused on media content even when their eyes appear to be glued to the screen or page. Misinterpretation is an important part of the process and the individual's ability to "get it wrong" needs to be accounted for in the equation through which we understand how people experience advertising in everyday life.

Ambiguity may be a technique by which advertisers attempt to gain viewers' attention. Although this may sound contradictory, ambiguity may indeed serve to elicit curiosity as viewers ask themselves: "What's going on here?" And, although viewers or readers may not "figure it out," they may, in the process, for a time give over their attention, if only partially, to the advertisement. In other words, they may consent to give into the wonder of advertising. The idea that individuals cannot quite figure out what is going on in the advertisement, or even that it is an advertisement at all (it is increasingly the case with magazines where it is difficult to differentiate the advertisements from the editorial content) has become an attention-getting technique. The irony, however, is that the advertiser has to trade off meaningful content that promotes the attributes of the product in order to gain the individual's attention. What is substituted for meaning is experience. In this sense, someone can derive aesthetic pleasure from the advertisement without finding much meaning or relevance in the message or product.

Some individuals have become so advertising savvy through their exposure to tens of thousands of advertisements that advertising agencies have come to use such techniques in order to fracture the expected form in which advertising appears. Fracturing the form—a magic trick of sorts—refers to a number of devices used by advertisers to make their commercial messages attractive in order to draw the attention of the viewer, reader, or listener. And, because fracturing the form is a way to break through the commercial clutter, the devices themselves must continually change.

The well-known Energizer Bunny commercial, that for a moment "tricks" the viewer into thinking she or he is watching something other than an advertisement for Energizer batteries, is one such example. The principal characters from the television program *Seinfeld* showing up in commercials for various products is another device. Conversely, products that show up in programming and movies are yet another device. This mixing of media forms—playing with structure, and so on—creates an intertextual web of advertising and popular culture.[6] The use of media figures and other cultural referents in advertisements is a means to build into a short commercial or one-page advertisement a social context in which to invoke the imagination of the consumer.

Ironically, one outcome of this meta-media, experienced many times daily, is that often individuals cannot remember very much of what they have read, heard, or seen. To that extent, advertising messages may not register or may sometimes confuse. As a result of the bombardment of advertising messages sometimes, for example, individuals refer to AT&T, the long distance telephone service as MT&T. Conversely they may refer to MCI, a competitor, as ACI. Getting it wrong or mixing up the name of a product is not merely a function of inattention, it is an important aspect of the way we "corrupt" commercial messages and in that a part of advertising as social practice. Twitchell (1996), too, pointed out that individuals will say the Energizer Bunny is advertising Duracell batteries, and he pointed to Taster's Choice and Pepsi commercials that have confused consumers.

Ambiguity and vagueness, it has been pointed out, are techniques available to the advertiser, a creative gimmick. Vagueness may tweak the emotions as the viewer or reader begins to ask through self-talk: "where is this taking place?" or "what is going on?" The multiple meanings may signify a way in which individuals get lost in advertising's magical world, and it may also signify one of the games individuals play with its content. Regardless, advertising play takes place in a distinct cultural and social space. In the process, sometimes the viewer, reader, or listener creates her or his own ambiguity. There is little the advertiser can do to control this. Placing the viewer in an ambiguous state tends to heighten emotions—more on the level of like and dislike, rather than love or hate—so that the end result is one that is emotionally shallow, and the advertisement's meaning may be ambiguous or vague. It is also possible the advertisement's content may or may not be salient to the consumer. The separation of meaning from experience in advertising is a postmodern phenomenon, and one that needs to be accounted for as we learn more about the work advertising does in the culture and the magic system in which it operates.

CONCLUSION

Fiske (1987) maintained that pleasure is derived from the extreme nature of some media content like that of advertising. The extremeness of advertising is rooted in the excesses of the medieval carnival. The pleasure that Fiske described comes from the opposition to "morality, discipline and social control" (241). Advertising, like the carnival, is an exaggerated play form. "Like play, carnival abides by certain rules that give it a pattern, but unlike play (whose rules tend to replicate the social), carnival inverts those rules and builds a world upside down, one structured according to the logic of the 'inside out' that provides 'a parody of extracarnival life' (Bahktin, cited in Fiske, 1987: 242). Consider, for example, both the 20th- and 21st-century versions of the Joe Isuzu advertising campaign in which the audience is in on the joke in this parody of the quintessential car salesman.[7] This particular campaign enthusiastically breaks the rules inverting the ideas of power and authority that individuals confront in their everyday lives. There is pleasure in this "empowering inversion" (242).

There are many devices, both visual and linguistic, available to the advertiser, in order to attempt to create meaning for the product in the mind of the consumer. However, the advertiser's ability to control meaning through the magical formulations within advertisements is limited. There may be much pleasure in experiencing advertising without converting that pleasure into a purchase. "Advertisements are seen, read, and enjoyed by millions of people who will never buy the commodity on offer" (273).

> Children, for instance, appropriate advertising jingles into their games, often subverting them by changing the words. Incorporated into children's culture, the advertising jingle bears very little, if any, of its original commercial meaning—probably not much more than nursery rhymes such as Little Jack Horner or Georgie Porgie retain their historical and political sense. The origin of a text neither guarantees nor determines its mode of reception, however powerful a party it may be in the process of negotiation (273).

Advertising in its excessiveness, goes beyond the products that are a part of its surface structure. Advertising is something we may experience; it is not merely a means of communicating the attributes of a product or service. An advertisement may be experienced directly by an individual and it may become part of a social experience outside of media consumption. As such, advertising transcends the information function that was part of mercantile exchange to become another element in our contemporary social world. Advertising still serves the interests of purveyors of goods and it has become, among other things, an ingredient in the social glue that binds us as a culture.

Advertising attempts to promote stability in a rapidly changing marketplace. One way it does so is through the enhancement and refinement of personal identity. The magic of advertising works when the individual in a "free-floating" world attempts to conform their "shape-shifting selves" (Lears, 1994: 9). It is, therefore, free-floating individuals in society who attempt to socially ground themselves and create a social identity, not necessarily through the acquisition of consumer goods, but by the ways in which they utilize advertising in their everyday lives. The acquisition of goods and services comes into play when an individual's desire to participate in the carnival of the marketplace serves as a symbolic act of empowerment. It may also be that advertising's role is to ground the free-floating individual, again pointing up its relation to stability—economic and social. There is simply greater comfort from a social and cultural point of view in being grounded.

The vision of the transcendent individual gives way to the image of the channel surfer dissatisfied with the advertisements flashing by on the page or screen. In other words, we have to allow for variations within the social practice of advertising in daily life. Such practices have been codified into neat controllable—cause and effect—schema that are a foundation of the dominant paradigm. A cause-and-effect relationship between advertising and consumers speaks of a controlled stable environment in which to conduct the business of commerce. It is important to remember that advertising is merely panoply for a relatively free and unstable market.

ENDNOTES

1. John B. Watson, the father of behavioral psychology, for a period of time in the 1920s worked for the J. Walter Thompson advertising agency.
2. Till and Shimp (1998) studied how negative celebrity information can affect the brand the celebrity endorses.
3. Tradition today is not the nuclear family, as the fastest growing segment in U.S. society is single heads of household. Advertisers adapt to the "new" traditions as they arise.
4. Consumer use of Internet banking and ATMs also means that banks can extend banking hours and employ fewer tellers, significantly cutting costs.
5. In a study of 2000 Super Bowl advertisements, researchers found that only 48% of respondents were able to identify E-Trade cor-

rectly as the advertiser even though they were able to recall the advertisement's slogan. Of respondents, 42% thought the E-Trade tagline belonged to another company (*Advertising Age*, 2001).

6. For an extensive discussion of advertising and popular culture, see Fowles (1996).

7. Actor David Leisure reprised his 1970s role as Joe Isuzu, the lying, smarmy pitchman for Isuzu trucks. In the debut commercial, "Joe throws his remote at his TV, snapping that Isuzu hasn't 'done a decent commercial since they cut me loose.'" In subsequent humorous commercials the character evolves into a more corporate "millennial Joe'" (Gornstein, 2001).

PART II

3

THINKING ABOUT ADVERTISING

MAKING, UNMAKING, AND REMAKING MEANING

An individual's discourse strategy of everyday life includes the social uses and private utility of advertising. *Private utility* refers to the ways in which individuals utilize their stream of consciousness and fantasy behavior as part of their ongoing internal dialogue. As individuals may be "away," in other words transported to another place and time during media consumption, there is a magical quality to this experience as the individual enters into a playlike, yet highly social, world.

This chapter is concerned with the ways in which the content of advertisements may become part of an individual's self-talk within the individual's imaginary social world. Stream of consciousness and fantasy behavior are considered a social practice, particularly when it takes place during media consumption. Advertising, because of its unique qualities, in terms of form, format, and function, make media consumption an ideal place in which to see how advertising does its work in the culture and the work we do with it. Furthermore, because advertising—both in broadcast and print—is a part of the flow from entertainment or news content, it presents an opportunity to take, literally and figuratively, a break from what is before us.

Caughey's (1984) research demonstrates a strong connection between stream of consciousness activity and popular culture. His informants reported streaming about popular songs, movies and advertisements. Caughey did not study stream of consciousness and fantasy activity during media consumption as streaming can take place during many routine activities from driving to work to performing routine tasks (Wallace, 1972). The routine nature of media consumption encourages individuals to enter into their stream of consciousness and fantasy behavior. Kubey and Csikszentmihalyi (1990) described the televiewing experience as an "altered state of consciousness" comparable to daydreaming (102).

Ang (1996) referred to fantasy as "a fundamental aspect of human existence" (92). She added the following:

> I want to suggest that the pleasure of fantasy lies in its offering the subject an opportunity to take up positions which she could not assume in real life: through fantasy she can move beyond the structural constraints of everyday life and explore other, more desirable situations, identities, lives. In this respect, it is unimportant whether these imaginary scenarios are "realistic" or not: the appeal of fantasy lies precisely in that it can create imagined worlds which can take us beyond what is possible or acceptable in the "real" world. (93)

Ang described the activity of fantasizing as a private practice that is available anytime, but one that individuals generally keep to themselves. It is, in other words, safe space.

When individuals are in their stream of consciousness, they are engaged in an imaginary social world in which they are replaying past experiences (memories) or anticipating "imaginative renderings of future experience" (Caughey, 1984: 125). The stream of consciousness takes place inside the "head" of the individual, but the interior world is a social world inhabited by familiar people, scenes, and situations, including media content with which the individual is familiar. When individuals are engaged in this imaginary social world they sometimes hear people including media figures, characters or popular songs or jingles while in the stream and they may engage in conversation with others within the stream. In the course of streaming, the individual engages in self-talk, a pervasive aspect of this process and social practice. As there is interaction within the individual's imaginings, the process is social, sometimes being talked to by media figures and sometimes talking with media figures (Caughey, 1984). Additionally, individuals participate in the stream of consciousness as a matter of routine behavior; it is an ordinary occurrence for which little credence is given. Nevertheless, such routine behavior is a pervasive aspect of American culture and media consumption in particular that is a significant dimension of the ways in which we experience advertising in our everyday lives.

Caughey maintained that action-oriented Western culture prefers to deny the stream of consciousness. After all, how can one be productive at work if involved in stream of consciousness or fantasy activity? Although capitalist ideology may hold disdain for this activity, it is universal. "It appears that people in all societies experience drifting sequences of memories, self-talk, and anticipations, but it also appears that people hold different beliefs about such experiences and that, to a degree, they may experience them differently" (Caughey, 1984: 129). Of specific concern to this chapter is the question: How can individuals actively process the content of advertisements while "away" in their inner playlike world? The stream of consciousness is governed by cultural knowledge and somewhat ironically, the stream does not whisk individuals away to some unknown territory, but rather focuses on Capitalist culture: We stream about name brand products, retail stores, and media, among other things. Even if individuals stream about some place where they have never been, it is likely they have visited this place through media consumption. Caughey said, "media material provides the imaginative building blocks" and provides evidence that the stream is "culturally constituted" (133). One of Caughey's informants reported anticipating in her stream a career in business and thought about a co-worker asking her for a date. She refers to the individual as "a handsome businessman like those in magazine advertisements." Media play prominently in the stream of consciousness. In addition to media figures, individuals may recall a favorite scene from a movie, or there may be a cue that drives the individual's stream to recall aspects of books or newspapers (Caughey, 1984).

ADVERTISING AND THE STREAM OF CONSCIOUSNESS

Writing about women's experiences of magazine advertising, Winship described (in Storey, 1993) the pleasure received from an advertisement without having intention to purchase a product. She said the following:

> We recognize and relish the vocabulary of dreams in which ads deal; we become involved in the fictions they create; but we know full well that those commodities will not elicit the promised fictions. It doesn't matter. Without bothering to buy the product we can vicariously indulge in the good life through the image alone. This is the compensation for the experience you do not or cannot have. (148)

This is similar to Radway's (1991) description of women who read romance fiction and the illusion they create for themselves. Ang (1994) countered that "If, however, we were to take fantasy seriously as a reality in itself, as a necessary dimension of our psychical reality, we could conceptualize the world of fantasy as the place of excess, where the unimaginable can be imagined" (520).

One of the major influences of advertising may be the appeal of object possession with actual possession of the object as the end goal. Caughey (1984) called this inward activity *mental commercials* in which individuals use the descriptions and language of advertising to describe their fantasies. "Fantasy descriptions of ideal houses often sound like commercials, and many can be traced directly to particular media productions (e.g., a California bachelor's pad to a layout in *Playboy* magazine). Like their media counterparts, these mental commercials characteristically embody the intense, quasi-sexual gratification that supposedly can be had from possession of luxuries" (176-177). He continued: "Often self-confirmation is received indirectly through imaginary others, as by winning their gratitude, admiration, or envy. This theme, incessantly employed in media advertisements, is regularly echoed in American fantasies" (177).

The stream of consciousness and fantasy behavior during media consumption is a ritual of practiced inattention. It is learned behavior, a practice to which we have, over time, become enculturated. The self-talk associated with stream of consciousness and fantasy behavior is a part of the dialectic response to advertising as individuals from time to time engage—through wonder and consent—with some of its content. As Krugman (1988) suggested, viewing television commercials presents "covert opportunities, with eyes-on-screen but thoughts elsewhere, and waiting for what comes next. It is perhaps the purest form of learned or practiced inattention" (49). Krugman concluded that turning attention away from a television commercial, for example, may be a form of silent protest. Practiced inattention is a discourse strategy when other defenses against advertising are not available, and advertisements may be a rest stop in which audiences, in a sense, catch their breath. It may be that looking at advertisements is not a very demanding task or an engrossing experience, conditions that will not sustain an individual's attention. Rather, audiences not fully taken by this experience are likely, under various conditions like seeing an advertisement over and over again, to shift their attention inward. Kubey and Csikszentmihalyi (1990) described watching the same television programs or movies as similar to hearing a fairy tale over and over. This, they say, "may offer the viewer a means of adaptation and a sense of mastery similar to dreaming the same daydream many times in response to daily frustrations" (103). They added, "As with a repeated fairy tale, repeat viewing can provide a stimulating yet ordered and comfortable experience for the viewer. This is one of the primary reasons that many people view the same television program or film many times" (103).

Familiarity, comfort and escapism are only partial explanations for the individual's involvement in the imaginary world during daydreaming. One of the functions of an advertising campaign is to communicate the selling message repeatedly, repetition being one of the basic tenets of effective advertising communication. There is, however, a major difference between the cooperative televiewing that might describe repeated exposure to a movie or TV program and the coercive manner in which advertising repeatedly forces itself on the audience. Advertising is one element in the flow of programming and editorial material, and audiences become adaptive to the content that is repeatedly put before them. Therefore, the ways in which individuals process the repeated advertisements and other media content together make media consumption a likely opportunity for daydreaming. It should not be assumed that daydreaming is a form of passive acceptance. Daydreaming and fantasy may be ideologically charged as "a compensatory domain" that empowers individuals who may not be escaping from the real world, but "acting upon it" (Fiske 1987: 317). Feshbach (1976) linked media consumption and the individual's inner world when he said, "in order to understand the influence of television and other media upon behavior, one need understand the function of fantasy activity." He continued:

> The fantasy experience provided by some television programs with aggressive content can control or reduce aggressive acting out behavior because the fantasy provides a substitute for aggression toward the actual target, because it provides an opportunity for the expression of anger, because it functions as a cognitive control, because it is satisfying and enjoyable, and because it may facilitate new insights and cognitive reorganization. (71)

Campbell (1987) acknowledged that advertisers promote the idea of daydreams by creating tension between anticipated and actual experience. Campbell recognized that "advertisers make use of the fact that people daydream, and indeed feed those dreams" (91). He emphasized that advertisers provide the material for daydreams.

> It is important not only because the individual has to actively use the words, pictures, and sounds to construct an "as-if" world for himself to inhabit, but also because the process of day-dreaming (which has in any case preceded contact with the cultural item in question) may well continue long after direct contact has ceased; images relating to a particular film or novel being brought to mind subsequently and broidered in pleasurable fashion. (93)

Storey (1999) supported this position when he said, "although cultural consumption is an active process, the essential activity of the consumer is in the imaginative process of seeking pleasure" (16). Fiske (1987) added that the individual constructs meanings through daydreaming activities of their own representations of the world. The difference between stream of consciousness and fantasy activity is that the former is quasi-realistic, whereas the latter is unrealistic. However, those differences are diminished when this inner activity is viewed from the point of view of culturally constituted representations that individuals create as a means of making sense of their world.

If advertising worked in the manipulative way in which critics claim and the controlled manner in which the industry believes, then it would be reasonable to expect the content of advertising to subliminally enter the unconscious to show up in fantasies and daydreams. It would stand to reason that advertising that violates us in this manner, as some critics have suggested, would surely show up in the individual's inner world. After all, the dominant view of popular culture is that it is escapist, and that it takes viewers, readers, and listeners away from the real world. This is just one of the reasons to debase it. The advertising industry does little to dissuade consumers from thinking about advertising's power on the unconscious as it sometimes plays with the notion of fantasy. A campaign for Sony Corporation, for example, wraps all of their advertising under the theme, Dream On. The corporation says it wants "to encourage more creativity, more joy and more dreams." The advertisements encourage the audience to retreat to "a place called Sony," which the advertising agency describes as "an emotional and physical metaphor." One of the television spots takes place in a toy and hobby shop. As the television commercial unfolds, the audience is transported to a whimsical world—a place called Sony. The intention of the advertisement is to induce a fantasylike experience. Indeed the voiceover says, with Sony products, "you don't watch TV, you feel it" (Elkin, 2001). In this fictive world of Sony, the individual is encouraged to enter into the imaginary sphere "to feel," that is to express his or her power. It is important to point out that the world of Sony is a world limited by its own history. However, it should not be assumed that individuals who choose to participate in that imaginary world are limited by the representations created and presented by Sony.

Advertisements, like the one just described, sometimes include fantasy sequences and may encourage fantasy behavior and contribute to the construction of thought and fantasy within the individual. In this sense advertisements may suggest what subjects are appropriate for fantasy and in what context it is appropriate to fantasize. Advertising, Schudson (1984) said, is set out of time and space. "Often commercials seek realism, but sometimes the aesthetic mode is surrealism, especially in ads for products like perfume, closely connected in the culture to dream, fantasy and desire" (1984: 216). This is an important distinction as only certain advertisements, like those for perfume or cologne attempt as a creative technique to evoke fantasy, whereas others, for example those for everyday use products like laundry detergent, may be more realistic in their "slice of life" approaches.

THE STREAMING PROCESS

There is a parallel quality to the ways in which individuals conduct social relationships and consume media. That is to say, in the midst of both situations, individuals may be "simultaneously 'away' in the imaginary social worlds of memory, anticipation, and self-talk" (Caughey, 1984:153). Media consumption, then, is like half listening to a conversation and is akin to multitasking. Caughey suggested that fantasy behavior is not an escape from the culture. Stream of consciousness "should be viewed as mental commercials for a materialistic value system" (186). This may account for a number of popular references used to describe media consumption in general or the consumers mental state as couch potato, hypnotized, and narcotized. Some research (Kubey & Csikszentmihalyi, 1990) reports how in the process of media consumption physical changes take place, like the tendency for the body to relax. Such physical changes do not indicate an altered state or hypnosis. Being in an altered state refers to media consumption as dysfunctional behavior, implying the audience is passive and unable to critically discern what is happening or, in some instances, what is going on around them as their stream of consciousness runs counter to what is before their eyes and the sounds they hear.

The question ultimately is not whether viewers, readers, or listeners are passive or active, but whether the content is significant enough to warrant their engagement. Television viewing and other forms of media consumption are akin to daydreaming in that both are effortless tasks with no compelling need to direct behavior toward a specific goal (Klinger, 1971). Not only is this supported by brainwave studies (Klinger, Gregoire, & Barta, 1973), from a behavioral perspective "both television viewing and daydreaming often seem to involve a blank stare" (Kubey & Csikszentmihalyi, 1990: 101). The blank stare suggests that viewing may be compared to a hypnotic state. However Kubey and Csikszentmihalyi concluded, "Under certain conditions, particularly during uninterrupted and extensive viewing, the television viewing experience might qualify as an altered state of consciousness" (102).

It is not so much that media consumption and stream of consciousness activity are dysfunctional, but the inner world has to a great degree gone unrecognized. As Caughey (1984) stated:

In our society fantasy has traditionally been viewed in one of two ways. First, like stream of consciousness processes generally, fanta-

sy has often been seen as "Woolgathering", an unrealistic, unimpor-
tant waste of time—and hence a trivial subject for research.
Alternatively, it has often been viewed as quasi-pathological activity,
a proper subject only for abnormal psychology and psychiatry. In
recent years both these assumptions have gradually been replaced
by an increased recognition of fantasy as a normal experience, having important functions for the maintenance of psychological equilibrium. (184)

As a leisure activity with little at stake, attending to commercial media and the advertisements that play a part in the flow of their
content, provides a forum in which the viewer or reader can, as Fiske
(1989) suggested, rework the content in order to create meanings of
self, social identity, and social relations. In this sense, Fiske posited
that tearing or disfiguring a commodity such as an advertisement
enables the individual "to assert one's right and ability to remake the
content into one's own culture" (15). This issue of power is important
to advertisers as such reworking of content may undermine the selling
of products to an audience that comes to media with a wide range of
potential tactics for consuming it and strategies for using it. The issue
is not about whether audiences are conceptualized as passive or active;
as pointed out earlier, the important question is whether the activity in
which consumers are involved is significant enough to warrant their
involvement. After all, how can audiences be expected to recall products advertised when they have been involved in daydreaming, fantasy,
or stream of consciousness activity? Clearly, such inward activity is
only a part of the individual's media experience, and advertising
research to a great extent has avoided the topic, concerning itself with
traditional measures of comprehension (e.g., recall tests or categorized
reactions to commercials).

The industry framework for processing advertising does not
account for fantasy activity because it cannot be controlled or predicted by the advertiser. Rook (1985), for example, suggested ritual
responses to advertisements are likely to trigger immediate behavioral
responses. But, as with passive and active viewing, this reductionist
orientation is just one of several contradictory paradigms that have
emerged regarding an audience's processing of and reaction to advertising. One view depicts an attentive viewer focused on the content logi-
cally processing information (Palmer, 1986), whereas another might
depict an individual who leaves the room when the commercials appear
only to return after they have ended and the programming has
returned (Anderson & Meyer, 1987). Advertisers have expectations of
how viewers, readers, and listeners see and experience commercials.
Advertisers expect individuals to be present, focused on the content,
and entertained by clever jingles or slogans, attracted by a celebrity, or

informed of the uniqueness of a product and its associated benefits. This assumes that the individual is looking to be entertained or informed and proceeds through a mapped out pattern of interaction. Creators of advertising utilize rapid, highly dramatic montages and unusual or improbable situations, unique sounds and voices, or eye-grabbing photography, through which they attempt to manage the individual's imaginative behavior. That is to say, the advertiser who beckons the individual into their fictive world, like the example from Sony, expects that individual to pay attention. However, it may be the very creative techniques used by advertisers, among other elements unique to advertising like repetition, that promote fantasy activity. The industry expectations do not account for Fiske's notion of reworking the commercial content. This reworking may be referred to as the individual's "regular route" through the commercial clutter and as such is a ritual practice that becomes a discourse strategy in the individual's social construction of reality.

Advertisers consciously use signs attempting to create, as P. Berger and Luckmann (1966) suggested, a shared reality. It is the symbolism as well as social roles, relationships, hierarchy, and so on depicted in advertisements that help to define that reality. Similar to the position offered by Rook, Solomon (1983) suggested a straight line between depiction of those symbols in advertising and ensuing behavior. This assumes that individuals who view, read, or listen to advertising are direct consumers of its content. However, Fiske (1989a) points out that individuals go beyond mere consumption, "treating content not as a completed object to be accepted passively, but as a cultural resource to be used" (10-11). Kubey and Csikszentmihalyi (1990) maintained, "because the mass media are themselves part of a cultural system, they present information within an interpretive structure (e.g., metaphors) that 'frame' news events as well as fictional treatments in line with the dominant political culture" (32). Therefore, the reworking of content to which Fiske referred takes place within a range determined by the dominant culture, in this case advertisers. Although not referring specifically to advertising, P. Berger and Luckmann (1966) similarly suggested there is an ongoing correspondence between the "originator's" meanings and "our" meanings. Advertisers rely heavily on metaphor as a creative approach. Metaphor, however, by its very nature falsifies facts, which may partially account for the ways individuals move between the imaginary world of advertising and their own imaginary world.

P. Berger and Luckmann (1966) refer to reality maintenance as one means of maintaining our mental well-being. Communication media play a role by reassuring us that things are as they seem. One of the ways to achieve this reassurance is through attention to the repetitive forces of advertising and perhaps connecting that content to something relevant in the viewer's life. An ancillary mechanism to help maintain that reality is through conversation. Berger and Luckmann, however, are concerned with interpersonal, not intrapersonal communication. Other forms of intrapersonal activity might include daydreaming or stream of consciousness—areas Caughey (1984) called "pervasive dimensions of human experience" (120). He suggested that, like interpersonal communication, stream of consciousness maintains connections to both cultural knowledge and social conduct. P. Berger and Luckmann (1966) described this participation in multiple realities as a play form that helps us make sense of reality and through which we develop a common sense about reality.

Stephenson (1967), too, argued that mass media provide a context for "pure play (of becoming) detached from real life . . . stepping outside the world of duty and responsibility" (46-47) and a "highly developed form of subjective play (which is) more like being in a trance" (50). Silverstone (1999) disputed Stephenson's theory of play, but did support the idea that play is a source of culture. "Play is pursued within a distinct and distinguishable social and cultural space. It is rule-governed but protected and differentiated from the rule-governed normality of other (principally work-related) spaces of the rest of everyday life" (Silverstone, 1994: 169). Important to the study of advertising in everyday life is that, as Silverstone said, "the boundaries between fantasy and reality are becoming less and less clear" (169). Although Silverstone added, the boundaries still hold. The notion of a "regular route" or the routine practice of everyday life is consistent with this viewpoint, as consumption of advertising is something individuals do routinely and advertisements repeated often include familiar scenes and characters. In line with this point of view, Kubey and Csikszentmihalyi (1990) reported that, "almost 90 percent of all reported thoughts about television occur while viewing" (78).

STREAM OF CONSCIOUSNESS AND ADVERTISING USE

The inner use of advertising is a private practice—a discourse strategy—that includes, among other actions and reactions, the potential to participate in stream of consciousness and fantasy activity.[1] Among the things that individuals think about when involved in an inward experience are memories and anticipations and associated self-talk. Consider the example of an informant watching a television commercial for Coca-Cola:

> The commercial started off by saying there was 6 weeks until graduation. Then the commercial continued to show five college students

> hopping on a subway to go to a concert. After the concert they get
> back on the subway. It's when they get back on the train they are all
> tired because they all fall asleep on each other. One guy looks
> around at his friends and says, "even though we were on a hot air-
> less train, I realized that this was the best night of my life—and a
> part of me wished that I could stay on this train forever and that we
> could always be together." I looked at my roommate who was watch-
> ing television with me and I thought how I wished I could be with her
> forever and how I don't want to graduate from college.

The Coke commercial is intended to elicit an emotional response as
part of a campaign intended to evoke sentimentality. It clearly accom-
plishes this goal, however, in this case the viewer both remembers a
shared past and anticipates a change that is about to take place in her
life—graduation and the person she will miss most. The commercial
itself, or rather some aspect of its content, serves as a cue to drive the
individual's stream. Once in the stream, the flow seems to take its own
direction. The viewer is no longer focused on the commercial, but is
involved in an imaginative rendering of her future. In another example,
an informant who, while watching a television commercial promoting
fried chicken for a fast food restaurant, engaged in the following self-
talk in anticipation of a job she describes as one she hated:

> I hate the smell of chicken! I hate working at Roy's too. It's a slave
> job! Oh shut the hell up! If you hated it so much, you wouldn't be
> there still.

The temporal connection to the commercial itself is important for generating this particular stream of consciousness, but the self-talk dominates the stream and is based on a strong emotion of a memory. As
demonstrated in both examples, Caughey (1984) suggested, "self talk
typically includes verbalized reflections of current, past and future situations" (126). The memories and anticipations represented by these
diverse examples do not depict highly imaginative and necessarily positive thoughts that are associated with a product or service. Rather, in
both instances, the informants anticipate something they dread.
Similarly, a woman watching a commercial for laundry detergent
reported a similar anticipation in her self-talk:

> I get so tired of people telling me what clean laundry is . . . I hate
> laundry . . . I hate everything about it. Why is it my job?

These examples indicate that within the internal dialogue there are
links between subjects that may be traced to cues within the advertisements. This is the nature of the flow of the stream of consciousness.

The stream itself reflects to some degree the flow between programming and its links to commercials and with regard to print, editorial matter and its links to advertisements. It is possible that the return to a program or turn of the page, for example, can serve to interrupt the stream and call the individual's attention back to the screen or page. In this sense, "media material provides the imaginative building blocks" for constructing the stream of consciousness (Caughey, 1984: 133).

These informants engage in self-talk that is similar to the way we, at times, talk to others. In addition, this self-talk about advertising is emotionally charged. Such inner experiences help to establish or maintain cultural knowledge about the external world as these descriptions depict events or situations that individuals experience in their everyday lives. Trying to find a connection between the self-talk the product/brand or some activity in the commercial is less important than establishing the fact that there is a greater social context in which this experience takes place. Most interestingly, the thoughts themselves move beyond those reactions anticipated by advertisers toward unanticipated connections to other aspects of the individual's life— their social world.

SELF-TALK BEYOND MEDIA CONSUMPTION

Advertising references show up in the individual's stream even when the individual is not consuming media. One informant reported the following stream while stopped at a traffic light:

> While sitting there I realized I had been singing (to myself) the jingle from the Miller Beer commercial—"When you've got the time, we've got the beer. . . ." When I realized what I was doing, I looked up at the car in front of me. I noticed that the guy in the middle of the back seat was wearing a painter's cap with the Miller logo on it. I rarely drink beer and never drink Miller beer.

And, another informant reported "Every time I drive by a McDonalds, I hear that damn jingle over and over again in my head." In another instance, an informant described how she is at work counting the time before she can go home. "I start thinking about how slow time is going by. This reminds me of a Mrs. Butterworth's syrup advertisement . . . 'nice and slow, she takes her time.'" And during a trip to the grocery store another informant describes the catch phrase from a bathroom tissue jingle that runs through her mind when she passes the product in that aisle.

Similar to these examples, informants report that certain aspects of advertisements, like slogans and jingles, stick in the mind. One informant reports how he couldn't get the song *Everyday People*, utilized in a Toyota mini-van commercial, out of his head. He says, I don't need a mini-van, and maybe I wouldn't even buy one of theirs if I did because of how much that commercial bothered me, but it did keep that company and its product in my mind. A high school teacher describes the following experience:

> I was surprised to find that I was not the only "weirdo" humming and singing commercials to myself. During a short quiz I overheard one of my students softly singing the words of the new Burger King jingle to himself.

Caughey (1984) found similar evidence that he described an "ominous" aspect of the insidious quality of advertising:

> I had been watching a lot of college basketball on TV, and they kept showing this one commercial for Roy Rogers Restaurants. It showed these super clean-cut and cheerful kids fixing hamburgers, and smiling Roy himself, all to the accompaniment of this song, which kept repeating the phrase "Say howdy to fresh food at Roy Rogers" . . . again and again. I must have seen that commercial thirty times, and found that even though I despised it, the song, or rather the phrase, kept running through my mind. . . . Yes, damn it, I did go to Roy Rogers during that period. (134)

MULTIPLE REALITIES AND ADVERTISING CONSUMPTION

As depicted in the following example, characteristics of the stream of consciousness are elements including anticipation (Valentine's Day); emotions (feeling romantic); and, talking to one's self (I ask, Why?).

> I'm watching this "diamonds are forever" commercial and it makes me think about Valentine's Day coming up. And I anticipate that they will be playing this commercial more. I feel romantic . . . caring. . . . Why?, I ask myself. That couple [in the commercial] really look to be in love with one another.

The stream may involve combinations of these elements as well as memories and other sensations. Another example begins with a memory, moves toward an anticipation and ends with an emotional reaction. In this case, a character in the commercial stimulates the thought:

> The man's body [character in an Absorbine Jr. commercial] is very
> muscular and it reminds me of my boyfriend's body, and I start think-
> ing about him leaving for Texas today. I get a sad feeling and think
> about how I'm going to miss him . . . we've never been apart before.

This is typical of the multiple realities experienced while consuming
advertising. In the inner world, relationships and emotions referred to
by informants are similar to those found in the objective social world
rather than some highly imaginative world of make-believe. That is to
say that informants did not describe in their stream of consciousness
driving an expensive sports car in some exotic local. There are brands
within their stream, but they are more likely to be Tide than Tiffany.
On the other hand, the appearance and relationship to celebrities in
stream of consciousness and fantasy activity are something else.
Rather, their descriptions were more likely to be closely tied to events
or situations in their everyday lives. A graduate student reports recalling a Pepsi commercial titled, "Pepsi presents Shaq in Hollywood."

> Shaq enters Hollywood after just being traded from the Orlando
> Magic and is living it up in L.A. when he realizes that something is
> missing and that it's Pepsi. The commercial didn't make me want to
> have a Pepsi, but it did get me to daydream about California. I
> remember seeing tall palm trees lining the street and the blue sky in
> the background—this makes me daydream. I have always wanted to
> move out to California and I begin to think how awesome it is.

As indicated by the descriptions provided by the informants, the inner
experiences of advertising are more likely to focus on the pragmatic
and situations close at hand rather than the fantastic or highly imaginative wanderings one might expect would be stimulated by viewing
highly imaginative advertisements. This is consistent with Caughey's
conclusion that the inner world of thought is culturally bound, but
goes beyond to suggest there is a connection between advertising-related stream of consciousness and pragmatic aspects of the individual's
immediate social world.

Additionally, as there are many potential ways in which individuals might rework the advertisement's content, no advertiser could
anticipate or include them all. And advertisers cannot work against the
pragmatic stream to evoke the kind of fantasy behavior they desire.
Therefore, the specific advertising content remains to a large degree an
open, polysemic, text. This is further illustrated by an informant
watching a commercial for a Kodak camera; one with a Christmas
motif. In his thoughts, the viewer anticipates shopping for Christmas
gifts. The thought may have nothing to do with the camera (in this
case) being advertised, but relates to an impending social obligation.

You know I just realized that Christmas is just around the corner. I wouldn't have been reminded until this [Kodak] commercial comes on. This Kodak disk camera commercial shows all these stuffed animals—they [the stuffed animals] would be perfect—and cheap—for my nieces and nephews.

Although the advertisement might provide ideas that would satisfy the anticipation, the evaluation is not necessarily of a pleasant nature. As noted already, some of the self-talk suggests a rather negative reaction in the individual's stream of consciousness when someone says, for example, "I hate laundry."

In addition to negative emotional reactions to the products or some related task, there are examples of informants referring in their self-talk to advertisements as "stupid," and "dumb." It is as though an inner debate is taking place in which the individual presents a statement about his or her situation—working in a fast food restaurant or doing laundry—and then responds to that situation. In the last example, the individual, perhaps overwhelmed by Christmas, reacts by exclaiming "Sheer Madness!" Part of the interaction between the individual and the advertisement is the potential for the individual to challenge the advertisement. In another example, an informant says:

The other day I was looking at *Cosmopolitan* magazine and I saw an ad that made me do a double take. The ad (for Candies shoes) featured pop singer Mark McGrath of the band Sugar Ray. He's standing in front of a mirror shaving, clad only in a towel (that looked like it was about to fall off) with a young woman standing behind him. I thought to myself, "what on earth does this have to do with shoes?"

In this instance, the informant, interacting with the advertisement, drifts in and out of a playlike world of stream of consciousness; as such advertising at times can be like a friend you cannot trust.

McCracken (1987) claimed in his meaning-based model of consumption that advertising invests cultural meaning in goods. But as these informants indicate, the connection may go beyond the benefits associated with those goods and services being advertised toward a connection with other aspects of the individual's social world. Meaning may be derived from something the viewer takes out of or puts into the advertisement, but meaning may—at least in some cases—only tangentially derive from the product. More likely, the cultural connection is to expected rules of conduct, values, and social relationships. Therefore, the meaning that is derived through their experience of and through advertising is culturally structured.

Although inward experiences take place alone within the individual's private world, descriptions provided by informants indicate that within the stream the individual may not be alone.

> I love to feel happy like those people in the 7-up commercial . . . they start dancing in the rain and I recognize that I'm smiling and laughing with them. It makes me feel really good. And I notice that I am laughing out loud. I think about the happy relationship between this man and woman and visualize my own relationship like theirs.

Here the individual reflects on a happy relationship between a man and woman; a social scene that indicates the imaginary world is a social world. The correspondence then is not just between the advertiser and the viewer, but rather the advertiser and the viewer's social world. Therefore, meaning is derived through a dialectic based partially on the advertisement's content and social scenes, settings, and individuals to which the viewer connects.

Not only do informants report anticipations while experiencing advertising in their daily lives, they also describe memories as diverse as the Vietnam War, childhood experiences, and family remembrances. For example, an individual viewing a advertisement for a chicken coating reports the following:

> I wondered why the little boy hesitated coming to dinner, and then as he explained why he didn't want the chicken coating crispier, I saw his teeth. I started thinking of when I was a just as little and didn't have any teeth and I couldn't eat corn and when I was in my teens and had braces . . . I couldn't eat crispy things.

In another example, the informant recalls a series of memories prompted by a commercial for Toyota automobiles. The commercial opens with a shot of a very long bridge.

> I wonder if this is the Seven Mile Bridge down in the Keys. I rode over that bridge 3 years ago on my honeymoon . . . a happy time . . . lots of hopes and the future.

When the commercial cuts to the interior of the car the individual reported renewed focus on the woman driver looking back over her shoulder to be sure the young child in the car seat was safe. In this case, the closer focus in the commercial actually helped her to focus more closely on the memory.

> During the last year of my marriage, I tried very hard and hoped to get pregnant. I wonder if having a child would have helped to save my marriage. I want to be back driving on that bridge. I want that baby seat in the back of my car.

The scene described by the individual is based on traditional American cultural roles. The construct of marriage/divorce and notions of motherhood are highly recognizable because they are culturally structured experiences. Perhaps as important the informant uses her response to the commercial as an opportunity to restructure her past. This restructuring is a way to help maintain her self-concept. Caughey (1984) suggested that memories are full of self-concern. "It is not merely that the individual replays past experiences he has witnessed or participated in; rather the self is the focus" (148). He added that this preoccupation with the self may be a culturally constituted process. The stream of consciousness may include recollections of friends, relatives, or celebrities as in the following description of a homemaker watching a commercial for Neighbor Care Pharmacy:

> It's nice to see Rudy Miller (a local TV news anchor who had left her job) again. She got a raw deal at Channel 11 . . . her baby is due in January; she already has two boys. I wonder if Laura Charles (a local gossip columnist) will write about her in her column. That reminds me: Cal Ripken's (short stop for the Baltimore Orioles) new baby is due this month . . . I haven't heard anything.

Imaginary scenes within the stream of consciousness parallel scenes, roles, values and rules given by the culture suggesting the inward experience of advertising is therefore a culturally patterned social experience.

CONCLUSION

The regular route through advertising clutter is a highly subjective experience, and when viewers, readers or listeners turn inward a cultural world unfolds; one bounded by memories and anticipations that revolve around familiar scenes, roles, and values. The strategy involved in stream of consciousness is a culturally learned strategy, as the individual reworks the content to deal with matters that they may be already highly familiar. The practice of being "away" when confronted with an advertisement is, under some circumstances, an inappropriate behavior as advertisers intend for audiences to pay attention to what is happening in the advertisement. There is an obvious economic basis for paying attention to the advertisements. After all, how can audiences become inclined to purchase products when they are mentally "zapping" the advertisements? Just as daydreaming during work is unacceptable in American culture, it is "bad for business" if audiences do not pay attention to the advertisements.

Whether a member of a targeted consumer group or not, individuals may still use an advertisement as a cue to enter their inner world. Therefore, whether an individual engaged with an advertisement enters the stream of consciousness and anticipates a negative experience also evaluates in a negative manner the product or service being advertised misses the point. The anticipation of Christmas shopping or doing laundry does, however, indicate a tangential relationship between the stream of consciousness and what is going on in the advertisement. Additionally, the fact that individuals think about socially appropriate behavior suggests that advertising related thoughts do perform a socialization function, that while not predictable, contributes to the social order.

Engagement with the content of an advertisement may take place within a state of mind that may be dreamlike, where the individual may be given to fantasize, daydream, about other things. The notion of reworking the content—making and remaking meaning—allows audiences to negotiate their way through advertisements sometimes paying attention while at other times not paying attention at all. This ongoing correspondence between advertising and the individual becomes part of their social world in that it is comprised of media figures, jingles, catch phrases and slogans, as well as scenes, roles, values, and rules given by the culture. Through this correspondence, or self-talk, advertising contributes to the social order by serving as a self-socialization mechanism. Although not referring to stream of consciousness (inner conversation), P. Berger and Luckmann (1966) pointed out that conversation is "the most important vehicle of reality maintenance" (152-153).

Fiske (1989) diminished the difference between fantasy and reality in that fantasy is a representation of what is real to the individual. He described the differences between reality and fantasy as two modes of subjective experience. The stream of consciousness is not merely a rest stop or a mental commercial, but rather "an important political part of popular culture (1989b: 125). As a political process, the stream of consciousness is an opportunity in which individuals may resist the text—in this case advertising—as it is offered. In this sense individuals use their daydreams as a means to oppose the dominant forces in the culture and society. Therefore, thinking while consuming advertising is a means of cultural resistance. In their stream of consciousness, sometimes it is evident that individuals are questioning advertising and the system in which it exists. But as a subjective modality, stream of consciousness behavior is an opportunity for individuals to claim their own reality.

Although it may appear as though the thoughts contained in the stream of consciousness are private and therefore highly individualistic, this process is actually part of a public one, as the thoughts are culturally constituted scenes, roles, values and rules that are part of the public domain. This suggests that from an advertiser's perspective some people may think about laundry as a result of viewing an advertisement for a laundry detergent. However, there is no guarantee that thought will involve a particular brand or that the thought will necessarily evaluate that scene depicted in the stream of consciousness in a positive manner. It may be the very repetition of advertisements and our familiarity with them that contributes to this process.

The linear nature of direct effects gives way to audiences that present a world that is complex; one in which advertising is a part of the system that guides them to make sense of their world. Advertising serves as a control and container for human interaction (Carey, 1989). Therefore, thinking about the content of advertisements confirms and adjusts the individual's subjective reality, a part of the inner conversation about things silently taken for granted. Such inner conversations, Berger and Luckmann maintained, keep our purpose before us and help maintain a sense of values. Focusing inwardly on the content of advertising may be a way of achieving equilibrium in a rapidly changing culture, but it may also throw order out of kilter, adding uncertainty as individuals challenge the advertisements as they reframe memories and rework their anticipations.

This chapter described and interpreted the meaning of advertisements as a product of inward experience. As advertising is a backdrop for other aspects of the consumer's life, attention to advertising content and pursuant self-talk is likely to relate to current concerns, memories, or evaluations of products, advertisements, or advertising in general. This is not to suggest these are the only things audiences think about. This is, of course, important for advertisers interested in reaching target audiences. But it is also of interest in the broader scheme of things as the inward experience of advertising is part of the individual's social construction of realty and helps the individual to make their way through the world. On the micro-level individuals use of advertising may seem like a form of empowerment. However, all of this takes place within a culture that is dominated by the advertiser.

On the macro-level, Schudson (1984) described advertising as "capitalist realism"—the official art of 20th century capitalist culture. As such it promotes an ideal vision of life that is embedded in advertisements and a vision that is pervasive. However, consumers of advertising pay attention to some of them, sometimes temporally moving toward an inward experience that may or may not directly relate to advertising's content. One of the ways in which individuals confirm their reality is through self-talk, reacting to the content and structural properties of advertising and thinking about their lives.

ENDNOTES

1. For an explanation of the ethnographic methods utilized to collect and interpret the thoughts and fantasies described in this chapter see the Appendix.

4

DREAMING, DREAM SHARING, AND ADVERTISING

Writing about the 1900 Paris Exposition, Rosalind Williams (1991) said, "it is neither necessary nor possible to catalog all the dreams exploited by modern business" (221). For Williams, the first Exposition of the 20th century was a watershed, as for the first time the exploitation of fantasy and dreams triumphed over science and knowledge. In contemporary society advertising is the "stuff" of dreams, but whether the content of advertising actually becomes a part of our imaginary dream world is another question.

This chapter describes the relationship between dreams and advertising. A foundation is presented for understanding dreams as a product of the culture and their connection to media. The chapter discusses the ways in which media figures, advertising, and advertising references are present in dreams, and it explores the role of media-centered dreams in the imaginary social world of the individual. The chapter describes the ways in which individuals recount their dreams to others based on the social rules of dream sharing. Within those rules, the chapter suggests there are variations in the ways that individuals share, or do not share, their dreams about advertising.

Individuals in U.S. society waver between two disparate cultural beliefs about dreams: Dreams mean something, or dreams mean nothing (Tedlock, 1992). This dichotomy reflects the importance of waking life versus the diminished value of dreams and dreaming. In contrast to American values, some other cultures hold dreams to be an important aspect of everyday life and are likely to be shared (Caughey, 1984; Tedlock, 1992). However, in U.S. society sharing dreams is not an ordinary form of public communication, as there is little reward for remembering one's dreams, much less presenting them to others. With regard to dreams, dream sharing, media consumption in general, and advertising in particular, these are parallel experiences that connect the individual's imaginary world to their waking world.

PARALLEL IMAGINARY WORLDS

When individuals are absorbed in a dramatic television program, movie, or engrossing magazine article or perhaps an advertisement, they are in some respects transported to another reality. Similar to the ways in which individuals enter the stream of consciousness or engage in fantasy while consuming media, when falling asleep "we move away from objective waking life" and enter the dream world (Caughey, 1984: 77). There is little dispute regarding the connections between media content and dreams. Kubey and Csikszentmihalyi (1990) said, "Night dreaming, too, can be compared to television viewing in that both can be conceptualized as visual fantasy activity closely tied to wish fulfill-ment" (102). These researchers claimed that the similarity between media consumption and day and night dreaming and hypnotic states "lead us to further posit that television viewing may often permit an adaptive regression" which they describe as a pathological return to "earlier levels of development" (102).

Shannon (1990) suggests, "Experientially, dreams are like movies that pass through one's mind while sleeping. The cinemato-graphic nature of dreams is such a truism that, on first glance, there does not seem to be anything about it that is worthy of discussion" (235). He claimed that dreams are cinemagraphic because they are enactments in which the dreamer is both the director and the principal actor. "Dreams are activities acted in the theater of the mind. As such they are reflective of the entire network of associations that the mind is" (241). Van De Castle (1994) wrote, "dreams and films share many common features: moving visual image, changes in setting and charac-ters, spoken conversations, perceptual distortions, temporal disconti-nuities, flashbacks. They even share a similar physical aspect: both are observed in the dark" (12).

Wood (1979) maintained that much television content repre-sents a "significant flow of collective dream materials" (519). Flow is a concept that also can be applied to the individual in their dream state. In describing the way we experience television as flow, Raymond Williams (cited in Fiske, 1987) referred to the stream of programming as "a continuous succession of images that follows no laws of logic or cause and effect" (99). Clearly, a part of that flow of material in both print and broadcast media is advertising and, whether it disrupts a flowlike state of mind or enhances it remains to be seen. Caughey (1984) said that his informants deny the influence of media in their dreams, but he maintains that media are a dominant motif in dreams. "The presence of such beings (characters from media) in the dream world may tell us more about the individual's media socialization than it does about his subconscious self" (91).

Wood (1979) presented the following similarities between dreams and media content that can be applied to advertising. He said both have a highly visual quality; are highly symbolic; involve a high degree of wish fulfillment; appear to contain much that is disjointed and trivial; have an enormous and powerful content, most of which is readily and thoroughly forgotten; and make consistent use—overt and disguised—of materials drawn from recent experience. Advertisements are, too a great extent, structured like dreams. Wish fulfillment, one of the basic tenets of dreams, is also the basis for much advertising. Images in advertisements are sometimes "dreamy." And sequences and pacing in advertising is also in some cases dreamlike. Furthermore, like their counterparts in the entertainment industry, creative directors, copywriters, and art directors may be considered some of the best dreamers in the culture.

Dreams have played an important part in popular culture. From soap operas to movies to literature, dreams have been used as literary devices. In the movie *Patriot Games*, for example, a key character, Jack, realizes who his stalker is during a dream sequence in which he plays back events and notices there is always a woman present. In other movies, dreams have saved characters' lives because past events are played back showing hidden facts not recognizable in waking reality. Another movie, highly infused with dreams is *Nightmare on Elm Street* in which this fictive world is obsessed with dreams and the nightmare for which the movie is named.

Robert Louis Stevenson used his dreams to create *Dr. Jekyll and Mr. Hyde*. And in Dickens' *A Christmas Carol*, Scrooge changes his wicked ways in deference to his frighteningly real dreams. In the same way that these writers created popular culture out of their dreams, so too do advertising creatives use their own dreams as the basis for creative ideas. As all of these types of creative individuals are a product of the culture, it is likely the content of their dreams is likely to be reflected in their creative work. In this quasi-circular process creative individuals attempt to feed back to viewers, listeners, and readers that with which they are already familiar, know, understand, accept, and find pleasurable. They signal to their audiences that advertising is a play form, and they signal the appropriateness, if not the importance, of dreams and dreaming in U.S. culture and society.[1]

The similarities between dreams, media content, and advertising suggests a process orientation: Advertising is a form of dream equivalence that parallels the imaginary world of nocturnal dreams. However, when we look at the world of nocturnal dreams, we find they primarily are concerned with everyday problems and situations. They generally are about the mundane rather than the phantasmagoric (Alperstein & Vann, 1997). The problem–solution format of some advertising much like that utilized in advertisements for household cleaning products, among others, is also like the dreams we have. Sometimes advertisements attempt to replicate dream sequences. Products as diverse as Snapple beverages, Kowasaki motorcycles, and I Can't Believe it's Not Butter Spray revolve around dream sequences. A Snapple beverage advertisement, for example, begins with a letter written to the company in which a consumer tells of his dream of being in a parade riding on the Snapple float. The commercial proceeds to depict the dream (in effect making the dream come true or rendering it visual) as the announcer reads the letter. And the butter spray commercial is an example of wish fulfillment wherein Fabio (a male model) shows up at a woman's (representing the idealized everywoman) home to wait on her hand and foot. And, print ads also can be dreamlike not only in their imagery, but in their references to dreams. A Starbucks coffee newspaper advertisement carries the headline, "When Coffee Dreams it Dreams of Chocolate." The subhead in the advertisement reads, "Together they're a dream come true." Just like dreams, some of the advertisements we read, view, or listen to in the media are meaningful, others meaningless: some frightening whereas others may be humorous. Some advertisements, like dreams, may affect us long after watching, reading, or listening and some advertisements have no impact at all; and although the memory of some linger through many years, others may be forgotten almost immediately.

A CULTURAL UNDERSTANDING OF DREAMS

Fine and Leighton (1993) presented a model for a social and cultural examination of dreams that may be helpful in understanding, among other things, the way the content of advertising might show up in the individual's dream world. They stated:

> With their lack of internal control, cultural specificity, presentation rules, and interpretability, dreams stand apart from individual dreamers. Because dreams occur regularly and nearly universally, but in culturally specific forms, they connect to social organization while still being internally generated. (99)

Caughey (1984) amplified this when he said that, "As soon as one looks ethnographically at the inner world of dreams, one is struck by the high degree of cultural patterning. To a large extent, dreams are structured by the dreamer's culture" (83). Or as Fine and Leighton (1993) put it: "The figures and events in dreams are those figures and events that we either know or know about; they nestle within our cultural lives" (98). In addition to familiar faces, the dream world also includes familiar roles, relationships, and social structure found in the waking world (Alperstein & Vann, 1997). That is not to suggest there is an exact replication of the individual's waking world in the dream world, but the preponderance of scenes and situations found in dreams tend to reflect the waking experience of the dreamer. "The dream world, like the world of media, is an imaginary social world" (Caughey, 1984: 90). Caughey said, "somewhat like a movie viewer identifies with an actor and hence becomes fully absorbed in the doing of the dream, the dreamer is in his own dream" (86).

MEDIA FIGURES IN DREAMS

One of the ways in which we can demonstrate the cultural connections between dreams and media is to consider the ways media figures, who occupy a large space in the daily lives—including advertising—of most Americans (Gamson, 1994), show up in the individual's dream world. This space that media figures occupy in everyday life is only partially a product of the amount of time individuals spend with mass media, as media figures have become an important part of the communication system through which we socially construct reality and work our way through everyday life (this subject is explored in chap. 5). This connection between media figures from television and literature and dreams begins in childhood (Beaudet, 1991). As media figures play a significant role in the everyday life of most Americans, it stands to reason that media figures play a significant role in the individual's imaginary social world, including the world of dreams. "Just as unmet media figures play important roles in the individual's waking imaginary experience, so, too do they often figure prominently in his dream experience. . . . The presence of these media figures puts firmly to rest any misguided notion that media experience is not deep enough to affect our dreams" (Caughey, 1984: 91). It may be true that media figures and other media content may sometimes be present in dreams, but this may not be so because of the "depth" of that content. I disagree with Caughey on this point, as the question of significance is highly variable among individuals and therefore it may not be the depth of the content that is important, but rather the significance for the individual that determines whether or not media content enters the dream world. Additionally, there are structural properties, like repetition, that also may affect whether or not media content finds its way into the individual's dream world.

As dreams are structured by the dreamer's culture sometimes they include distortions, including bizarre characters. With regard to characters in the dream, Caughey (1984) maintained that "strange dream figures" are associated with the individual's media consumption.

> Zombies, vampires, prehistoric animals, animate computers, blob monsters, and talking rabbits are not to be found in the real world, but they abound in the fictional worlds of the American media. (1984: 91)

Members of the dreamer's family make up a high percentage of dream characters. In their classic study of dream content, C. Hall and Van De Castle (1966) reported that we dream about family members because these are the people with whom we are emotionally involved and about whom we have mixed feelings of affection, antagonism, and unresolved tension. "We dream about the people who are associated in some way with our personal conflicts" (C. Hall & Van De Castle, 1966: 33). In contemporary society, emotional involvement extends beyond friends and family to include "never met" media figures. Caughey's research confirms that some individuals do become emotionally attached to select media figures (see chap. 5). Therefore, it can be concluded that just as friends and relatives would likely show up in dreams, so too will media figures be present in the imaginary social world of the individual. A dream has a cast of characters, which can be classified by age, gender, and relationship to the dreamer and these include dream figures that connect waking imaginary experience to the content of the media world, including advertising.

In Caughey's (1984) study almost 11% of his informants' dreams contained media figures. As Caughey pointed out, when a media figure is present in someone's dream it is only occasionally that they are there in the role of celebrity. And he goes on to say, "when the interaction begins as that of celebrity to fan, the dream relationship is likely to develop into a more familiar form of interaction" (93). In addition to media figures, dreams contain social relationships, social roles, social structure, and social rules that are reflective of the individual's waking world, and reflective of the world of mass media (Caughey, 1984). In a study of media figures in dreams, Alperstein and Vann (1997) found that almost 57% of the informants who responded to a questionnaire said they recalled having a dream about a media figure; some appeared in advertising. They are almost always a male, from television (George from *Seinfeld*), music (Elton John), or film (Christian Slater). The sample of dream reports collected for the Alperstein and

Vann study (1997) include diverse media figures such as, Janet Jackson, Oprah Winfrey, Michael Bolton, Tim Burton, Jim Morrison, and Oliver Stone. However, the dream reports analyzed in the Alperstein and Vann study indicate that 8% of the sample had dreams that included media figures.[2] This finding is consistent with the results of Caughey's research. It is interesting to note that C. Hall and Van De Castle (1966) found that 1.3% of their dream sample were of "unmet prominent persons."[3] The disparity between the two findings in the Alperstein and Vann study reflects the difference between the actual representation of media figures in a sample of dreams (8%) versus the expectation that individuals have regarding the likelihood that that they would dream of a media figure (57%).

When media figures appear in dreams they are more likely to be friends or in some way interacting with the dreamer. And although they are recognized in the dream as a celebrity, their social role is altered in the dream world. The following dream provides an illustration:

> I am in a coed public high school that I have never seen before. I'm in homeroom and I don't know any of the people in the room so I don't talk to anyone. My clothes are very plain and I'm wearing my glasses and my hair tied tightly back in a ponytail. Looking over my notes, I get very agitated because I can't remember what I'm reading and I have a quiz on the material in my next class. Suddenly the door opens and the cast of the television program *Beverly Hills 90210* walks through the door. Apparently, they had all transferred and were now in my class. Tori Spelling, who plays my favorite character on the show, sits down next to me and starts talking to me. We become instant friends. She tells me all about her life and how lonely she feels because people only want to be her friend because she's famous. And I tell here that I've been feeling out of place because my family just moved to town and I didn't know anyone yet. She invited me to a party at her house in Beverly Hills later that night. Even though it's a school night my parents let me go because I pleaded with them. I arrive wearing a short sundress from Express and my hair is long and curly, like Julia Roberts, and I feel like I look really pretty. Tori introduces me to her friends and I feel completely at ease. I have no problem making small talk. Jason Priestly, another actor on the show, asks me to dance and we do. We got along great and he asks me for my phone number. I happily give it to him and he calls me the next night. He drives me to school the next day in his red convertible BMW. The dream ends with me being back in homeroom with my new friends and my new look. And I feel completely happy and at peace.

In this dream it is interesting to note that in addition to the several media figures mentioned, there are a number of cultural references to: fashion and style, specific products, and brands like a "red convertible

BMW" and "a sundress from Express." In the following dream, celebrity, Brooke Shields, appears as a member of a trio suggesting there is an understanding of social relations and social rules in the dream world. In the dream, they are driving around intoxicated after a wedding. There is awareness that driving while intoxicated is problematic.

> I had a dream that my roommate, Laura, Brooke Shields, and myself were driving around in a red convertible after a wedding reception. All three of us, dressed to the hilt, were a little tipsy. The mini crisis of the dream was that Brooke was trying to drive but was having a difficult time because of the effects of the alcohol she had consumed at the reception. We did not view this as a problem but rather as a hilarious form of entertainment. We were laughing the entire time. The dream ended after we pulled into a parking lot and turned off the car. Brooke could not restart it, so we laughed.

In addition to familiar faces, the dream world also includes roles, relationships, and social structure typically found in the waking world (Vann & Alperstein, 1994). That is not to suggest there is an exact replication of the individual's waking world in the dream world, but the preponderance of scenes and situations found in dreams tend to reflect the waking experience of the dreamer.

Another informant reports a dream that followed a discussion with her boyfriend after they had watched the television program *ER* together. The informant recalled telling her boyfriend "I would not throw George Clooney out of my bedroom if he suddenly appeared at 3 a.m. which, by the way, upset my boyfriend so I had to retract the statement."

> I was at a picnic in sunny California (a state I've never visited), and found myself sitting at a very long picnic table with gorgeous people discussing the woes of dating in Hollywood. Across the table from me, and two people down, was George Clooney, who began flirting outrageously with me. Soon he meandered over to my side, and started asking me out. Oh, the thrill of it all. Did I pursue this? Was my normally PG-rated dreaming about to take an "R" rating, or even better, an "NC-17"? Nah. I explained to Mr. Clooney that he lived in the fast lane, dating a gazillion gorgeous women all the time, and I was merely some faze he was considering—dating an unworldly, unjaded, not-so-incredibly gorgeous, normal woman from Baltimore. He persisted, but I held my ground, saying I'd stick with my Baltimore-based beau and wished him well in his romantic pursuits.

The dream itself may represent what Freud referred to as day residue, elements of the day that enter the dream world. Other informants reported hearing a media figure's name on radio or watching a movie in which that media figure appeared just prior to their appearance in the dream. The informant who dreamed of George Clooney reports that the next day, "I yelled at Keith [her boyfriend], saying that it was bad enough he didn't want me dating others in real life, but now his damned restrictions had entered my dreams, and that ticked me off, because one should be able to date others in his/her dreams."

Sometimes dreams affect waking life and as in this case emotions experienced in the dream show up the day after, affecting mood and perhaps behavior. Freud referred to this dream effect as *dream residue*. Again, other informants reported their dreams at night affected their moods or behavior during the day. "I had dreamed of Sting [the popular singer] on Friday night in which he was a neighbor who I spent a lot of time conversing with. He was like a friend to me." She says the next day after the dream, "I decided to listen to his band, The Police." The individual's daytime experience, including media consumption, affects dreams and conversely, dreams may affect the way we experience the next day.

ADVERTISING REFERENCES

There is an intertextual quality to media figures appearing in entertainment, news, and advertising. In other words, Jason Alexander first achieved celebrity status through his character George on the sitcom *Seinfeld*, that later translated into his spokesperson role for Rold Gold pretzels, among other products. Like many other media figures, he is an integral part of the communications system that fuels our dreams. This connection to advertising is not, however, the only type.

Of the informants in the Vann and Alperstein (1994) study, 19% indicated they dreamed about a television commercial, either being in the commercial, watching a commercial, or of an advertised product. As an example, one informant reported being in a commercial where everyone had huge smiles and remembered thinking "how fake everyone was." Another reported watching "weird" commercials that "didn't make any sense," and several informants reported appearing in advertisements. In one example, an informant dreams she becomes famous as a result of being in a commercial. The dream, she says, does not relate to a specific product or advertisement, but she is adamant about the relationship between being in a commercial and becoming famous. Another example involves a dream in which the informant writes and produces a McDonalds' jingle. In the dream, the informant's ability to write and produce leads to fame and fortune. And another dream involves a romantic liaison:

> I dreamed I was in a Close-Up toothpaste commercial; the one where they show couples kissing. I was in the advertisement with this handsome man and he was really thrilled about kissing me because my breath was really fresh and my teeth were clean.

In the following dream, the individual connects his dream to a bit of day residue from a television commercial:

> I dreamed that I was on the set of *ABC World News Tonight with Peter Jennings*. Jennings was lamenting that he was going to have to interview The Rock, a popular wrestler and movie star. Jennings felt he was pandering to the brass at Disney that owns ABC. But at one point he and I realize that it was AOL-Time Warner that own wrestling (whether this is true or not, I don't know). Jennings began to interview The Rock after the commercial break was over and he asked when The Rock was going to get back to wrestling and stop making movies, something his fans would like. I realized after I woke up that 2 days prior to this dream my son had said to me, while we were watching a commercial for an upcoming movie, that he wished The Rock would stop making movies and get back to wrestling.

In response to a question regarding whether the individual had an advertising-related dream, the Alperstein and Vann (1997) study elicited an interesting response. Informants reported that "I must have had a dream about advertising, but I just can't remember it." Such a response reflects the popular belief about the likelihood of dreaming about advertising. This response reflects a cultural expectation and social understanding of the way advertising and perhaps media in general works. Such a belief, however, is not reflected in the dream reports. Neither media nor advertising holds a dominant place in the dream world of the individual. Informants report that from time to time, slogans from advertisements show up in dreams, as do specific products, which may be a residual effect of advertising and serve as cultural referents when recounting dreams. Informants also report they may have appeared in an advertisement.

PRODUCT REFERENCES

An important element of advertising is its use of culturally loaded language to connote meaningful associations (Meyers, 1994). The meanings in advertisements are never neutral, but are used to mean different things to different people in different situations (Meyers, 1994). As in the examples just given, when individuals tell dreams to others they utilize language that will create meaningful associations. This is most evident when dream reports are viewed through their use of advertising inspired associations. Dreams, for example, may sometimes refer to cars, food, and drinks, and they are also likely to be peppered with widely advertised brand name products like: Fritos, Kentucky Fried Chicken, Wheaties, Heinz ketchup, Budweiser beer, Jeep Cherokee, and Champion sweatshirts. These referents are an important part of the dream world and are a means to convey meaning through dream recounting. However, advertising or particular advertisements did not show up to any significant extent in the informants' dream reports. Only one advertising slogan that referenced an obscure juice commercial was present in a dream. The slogan: "Florida grapefruit juice is pure, natural and good." Caughey (1984) found that although the settings and objects in dreams do not mirror the waking world of the individual, they do directly parallel the dreamer's waking cultural experience. "The dreamer is not in some strange never never land, he is in an American house with a screen door and a back yard in what turns out to be Baltimore, Maryland. This is characteristic of most American dreams. They take place in culturally constituted scenes drawn directly from the individual's experience of American society" (84).

As the dreamer is both the director and actor in his or her own dream, "they operate with ordinary knowledge drawn from waking social experience" (Caughey, 1984: 87). Sometimes, informants may report they have a dream about driving a car or wearing a red dress, but other times they are very specific like in the case where the informant drives a red BMW convertible or is wearing a Versacé designer dress. In this sense, the individual is acting within the categories of the culture's knowledge system, and a significant part of that system is the world of advertising that lends specificity to objects allowing the dreamer to experience the dream similar to waking life.

DREAM SHARING

An important end product of the process of dreaming is that of dream sharing. Dream sharing is a complex social process in which the individual has to recall his or her dream and decide—based on social rules and conventions—whether to share the dream or not and with whom to share the dream or not. In Vann and Alperstein's (2000) study, dreams were primarily shared for the purpose of entertainment. This was not only true for those who were telling the dreams (that it is their obligation to entertain), but also an expectation on the part of those being told dreams (they expected to be entertained).[4] Entertainment value does account for some of the reasons why dreams are shared. And entertainment provides a partial explanation why individuals' dream reports are full of cultural referents like name brand products, media figures and other media references. Individuals sometimes will describe the action in their dream reports using media-centric language like "the scene changed" or "in the next scene." In one example, the dreamer says, "The dream sequence was interrupted like a commercial break." In other descriptions, media analogies like, "the mountain was flat on this side, like the backdrop of a movie," or "the bar looked like the one from Cheers" are used when recounting the dream.

However, Americans do not share all types of dreams with others. Most informants (78%) in the Vann and Alperstein (2000) study felt there were unsafe situations in which to recount dreams to others. These reasons are bound by cultural rules and convention. Men, for example, would not share a dream that disclosed weakness on their part and females would not share a dream in which they had done something wrong. One informant says, "It would be unsafe if it reflects a hidden truth about yourself, something you don't want anyone to know."

This filtering of dream material suggests there are other situations in which an individual would not want to share a dream, situations including those that might show the dreamer to be overly materialistic. In dream sharing, individuals engage in what Goffman (1959) referred to as protective practices, strategies usually employed to enable the other to maintain face. In this sense, although the institutional context, like friendship, is a safe zone in which it should be safe to tell a dream, protective practices may ensure that safety by prohibiting certain kinds of dream recounting, like relating a sexually oriented dream. This also may be the case for advertising-related dreams. Although there are gender differences as to why individuals might not share their dreams, the fact is that as a defensive and protective practice not sharing a dream is an important aspect of self-presentation in everyday life. Not sharing an overly materialistic dream, for example, may be a protective practice, but peppering the recounting of a dream with advertising-related language may serve to reduce anxiety within the dynamic of the social situation in which the dream is shared, and make the experience more entertaining.

CONCLUSION

It is somewhat paradoxical that dreams of individuals heavily socialized through mass media would include so few media figures, so little programming and references to advertising that would at least be somewhat reflective of the extent to which they were involved with mass media. Or, to put it another way, would it seem likely that a medium that puts many of us to sleep—commercial media—would also become the content of dreams? Although most individuals say they have dreamed of a media figure, media figures were actually present in only eight percent of the dream reports, which is slightly less than reported in recent research. And, references to advertising were miniscule.

Vann and Alperstein (1994) found the nature of interactions in the dream world to be structured by the social rules of U.S. society. They suggested, "hierarchy transcends the real world to enter the dream world" (19). They furthermore suggested that rules governing this interaction follow this hierarchy: fathers tell daughters what to do, bosses manage employees, and police officers arrest law-breakers. This appears to be so with the exception of one category of individuals—media figures. When media figures, including prominent people like the president of the United States, are present in dreams they are the only dream figures whose status is consistently altered. That is to say, when a celebrity or prominent figure appears in a dream, they are more likely to do so as a friend, collaborator, or associate rather than in their role as celebrity. In the dream world, media figures are recognizable, but their social interactions, social relationships, and social roles change within the dream world. They are the only individuals in dreams to consistently lose their social status. This is what Caughey (1984) found in his study of dreams of media figures. On the face of it, this would seem unusual. However, Langer (1981) provided further understanding of this phenomenon when he distinguished between stars and personalities. The latter have a familiarity that offers their fans a much more intimate, equal relationship. He suggested that personalities are merged into their characters or submerged by them. He cited J.R. Ewing and the actor who portrayed him in the television show *Dallas* as being indistinguishable. Although Langer referred to our waking experience of media figures, such imaginary social relationships with media figures follow these same "rules" within the dream world. Therefore, these altered relationships should not be viewed merely as the media figure's diminished status. And they should not be read as an indication of our never-ending desire to be closely connected to such prominent individuals. In the latter interpretation in the dream world we can be friends with media figures, something that is not likely in the waking world.

One explanation for the small number of media figures and advertising references in the dream reports would be that media experiences are not deep enough to affect the unconscious. Perhaps more likely, the responses for media figures in dreams (Alperstein & Vann, 1997) may be accounted for as a product of cultural expectations on the part of the informants. That is to say, isn't it likely that we would dream about advertising? Individuals clearly understand they live in a mass-mediated culture that fuels this expectation. An alternative explanation presented here is that the structure of much media content is in itself dreamlike and therefore it is experienced already as an imaginary world, therefore, in the context of media consumption advertising does not show up to any great extent in the individual's dreams. Of course, this could also be a function of the amount of time the individual spends with mass media.

Freud describes how civilization is frustrating in that individuals have to suppress their impulses in order to live cooperatively. Dreams are one arena in which individuals can act out those frustrations abandoning the restrictive rules of society. For example, aggressive dreams, Caughey (1984) posited, are one indicator of the frustrations and problems of particular American roles.

> Here again there may be an important media connection. The world of media is better than reality; in the media, basic American values—grandiose career success, romantic and sexual fulfillment, warm family relationships, happy friendships, and material affluence—are intensely realized. This unrealistic vicarious fulfillment probably contributes to a sense of discontent with the more modest levels of satisfaction to be found in the actual social world. The frustration created by the gap between media fantasy and social reality may well contribute to the aggressive structure of American dreams. (106)

As advertising may be referred to as "pre-sleep stimulus," it may perform an adaptive function within the dream world of the individual. The repetition of advertisements serves a compensatory function in that the highly familiar scenes, situations, characters, and so on, reduce tension; therefore there is no need to dream about advertising.

Caughey's explanation is psychoanalytic and there are alternative cultural explanations that may better account for the limited presence of advertising content in individuals' dreams. From a cultural, perspective Fiske (1987) maintained that popular culture, and in that advertising, is a provoker of meanings. "Its commodities, which we call 'texts,' are not containers or conveyors of meaning and pleasure, but rather provokers of meaning and pleasure" (312). Fiske assigned much power to the consumer and referred to the "repertoires" of products that producers market to consumers on the basis of the unpredictability of success. Cultural resistance, therefore, is a means by which individuals resist the power of producers to convey meaning. Play, Fiske said, is a "source of pleasure" and is a "source of power" (315). He referred to the way children use the catch phrases of commercials and how they use the content of media in their fantasies to create an "oral and active culture out of the resources it provides" (315). Whether it is cultural resistance or a kind of tactical creativity as de Certeau (1984) described it, the kind of dream filtering described in this chapter is an important aspect of dream sharing in which individuals selectively choose to share their dreams about advertising and other culturally loaded material.

This chapter presented a few incidences where individuals described the use of advertising in their dreams. And it has presented a somewhat larger number of dreams in which individuals describe relationships with media figures. But there is little evidence that the dream world of the individual is infested with advertising, media figures, or product references. One explanation, and it is somewhat speculative, is that individuals choose not to tell about dreams of advertising because it is a way to demonstrate they are not cultural dupes at the mercy of marketers of products and services. We know from other research (Vann & Alperstein, 2000) that individuals filter a lot of what they dream. That is to say, individuals are very selective with regard to which dreams they will recount to others and to which others they will recount their dreams. It is likely that there is little cultural currency in sharing advertising related dreams, at least not as much currency as telling a dream in which a media figure appeared. When informants utilize name brand products in their dream recounting, they are using them as cultural referents, a means to make their own dream texts clearer in the way they communicate meaning. The uses of cultural referents in dream recounting are also a way to make the dream seem more entertaining, a primary goal of dream recounting. If advertising is the site of a cultural struggle, then resistance can take many forms. Choosing not to tell a particular dream or choosing to include some cultural referents and excluding others is just one.

There is no singular blanket resistance, but a huge multiplicity of points and forms of resistance, a huge variety of resistances. These resistances are not just oppositions to power, but are sources of power in their own right: they are the social points at which the powers of the subordinate are most clearly expressed. (Fiske 316)

The dream world is much like the culture of the dreamer's social environment that includes, but is not limited to advertising, movies, television and music. But it is worth emphasizing that these are perhaps parallel imaginary worlds—dreams and advertising—that sometimes cross, but are not so interrelated or intertwined that media becomes a predominant force within the individual's dream world. That is to say, dreams are reflective of the fluidity of the social and cultural structure of the dreamer's waking world.

It has been said that the world of mass media is like a dream world and as such is reflective of the collective unconscious of society. The world of mass media, and in that advertising, is reflective of the collective unconscious of society rendered transparent for all to see. Such a position assumes a rather homogeneous culture in which everyone attends to the same mass media content. But rather than being "collective," both imaginary worlds are segmented. In the same manner that entertainment is geared toward a particular subculture, elements of advertising and mass media that show up in dreams are reflective of particular subcultural interests. It is Jim Morrison of the Doors who appears in a Gen-Xer's dream to give advice, not Bing Crosby. This suggests that different subcultures within the society have different mythic needs as exemplified in the media figures with whom they are involved and who are likely to show up in their dreams.

The imaginary world of commercial media is present in the imaginary social world of dreams. It is not present in a way that dominates the dream world, but is reflective of the nature of the media consumption experienced by the individual dreamer. As with waking fantasies, the interplay between media and advertising content and the dream provides social utility beyond the dream itself as the properties of mass media—characters, programs, stories, and structure—may be used in the social context of dream recounting. Considering the presence, albeit somewhat limited, and nature of mass media and advertising content in the imaginary social world of dreams provides a view of the complex relationship between advertising and culture, in particular of the social utility of dreaming as a product of the culture in which we live.

ENDNOTES

1. The signaling to the audience that dreaming is appropriate in connection to advertising represents a contradiction in that dreaming during media consumption prevents individuals from processing the content. At the same time, advertisements promote dreaming, the "rules of media consumption" discourage individuals from entering the imaginary world of dreams during media consumption. Ironically, many people use television to drift off to the world of sleep and dreams or they read as a precondition to falling asleep.
2. Refer to the Appendix for a description of the methodology utilized to collect and analyze data reported in this chapter.
3. The difference between C. Hall and Van De Castle's (1966) research findings regarding the presence of media figures in dreams and more recent research may be reflective of the growth in significance of media figures since the 1960s.
4. Vann and Alperstein (2000) reported that 49.8% of their sample thought the purpose of sharing dreams with others was for entertainment. And they found that 50.9% of their sample believes that the purpose for telling dreams was to be entertained.

5

THE IMAGINARY SOCIAL WORLD AND USE OF MEDIA FIGURES IN ADVERTISING

In order to be a member in good standing of U.S. society, one should possess information about people one has never actually met, including knowledge of media figures. Caughey (1984) described the importance of such knowledge:

> In Europe during World War II, strangers dressed in American uniforms and speaking fluent English might be Americans lost from their own units or German spies. Standard interrogation questions designed to test American affiliations included inquiries about persons the individual could not be expected actually to know—for example, 'Who plays first base for the Philadelphia Phillies?' Answering such questions successfully was literally of life or death significance. (31)

The knowledge of media figures—individuals with whom we are familiar, but have not actually met—is an important part of everyday social interaction and distinguishes outsiders from insiders in U.S. society (Allen, 1982). In addition to knowing about media figures, people feel strongly about them. "People characterize unmet media figures as if they were intimately involved with them, and in a sense they are—they engage in pseudo-social interactions with them" (Caughey, 1984: 33).

This chapter describes the nature of imaginary social relationships with media figures appearing in advertising. It is concerned with the degree of connectedness to media figures that may range from mere awareness to deep and abiding loyalty. The ways in which individuals utilize those connections to media figures, not necessarily as a basis upon which to make decisions about products, but rather to mediate their imaginary relationships, is discussed.

MEDIA FIGURE FUNCTIONS

Klapp (1964) claimed media figures perform three major functions for their audiences. "First, they function as an emotional outlet providing a portal for both positive and negative feelings to be vented. Second, they function as role models that an individual may incorporate into his or her own make-up. Third, media figures may influence individuals to behave in certain ways; live in a particular lifestyle, for example" (34). The model through which media figures emerge, which Klapp referred to as a dialectic, does not identify why someone becomes a media figure; some people become media figures even though they would rather not. The celebrity-making process takes place in the form of a public drama that is in constant flux as new faces regularly appear on the scene. Advertising is an ideal, if not likely, place for this drama to occur.

Fowles (1996) described four ways in which individuals regard media figures in advertising. First, media figures "encapsulate and personify the normalizing services of popular culture" (117). By normalize he meant both to satisfy emotional needs and to confirm social norms. Second, individuals overlay the repeated exposure of the media figure with certain personality traits. In this sense, individuals reintegrate the media figure into their own lives through the idealization of certain qualities they appreciate. Third, individuals can utilize the media figure as a talking point in social discourse. And, fourth, Fowles suggested that media figures are a means by which individuals celebrate the world of popular culture, a world that is elevated from the mundane qualities of ordinary life.

Although interaction with media figures may take place in various media contexts, the ever-changing nature of advertising, and the dramatic conventions on which it is based (Esslin, 1987), make advertising an ideal place for this interaction to occur. Consider, for example, the consumer who is a long-standing fan of Jerry Seinfeld, whose imaginary social relationship grew through his long-running sitcom and who obtains an American Express card because Jerry Seinfeld is a guy you can "trust" and a "good guy." The importance of this pseudosocial interaction and evidence regarding the functions of celebrities from cultural (Caughey, 1984; Schickel, 1985; Schudson, 1984; Zeitlin,

1979), and marketing perspectives (Joseph, 1982; Rubin, Mayer, & Friedman, 1982) is well documented.

MEDIA FIGURES AND EMULATION

The use of testimonials by advertisers dates back to their unsavory connection to patent medicines in the 19th century. In the 1880s, the British company, Pears' Soap, used the concept of association—connecting cleanliness and godliness to their product—by obtaining an endorsement from U.S. preacher Henry Ward Beecher. Pears' later created an emotional connection to the product by having the actress Lillie Langtry endorse Pears' (Twitchell, 2000). However, it was not until the 1920s that advertisers featured famous people as product endorsers. Actresses Joan Crawford, Clara Bow, and Janet Gaynor were among the first celebrities to promote products (Fox, 1984). At that time, the rationale given by advertising agencies for using celebrities was "the spirit of emulation" (90).

The rise of performers as cultural figureheads is largely a 20th-century phenomenon that parallels the rise of popular culture and advertising (Fowles, 1996). The star system from which the early endorsers emerged was closely tied to the growing popularity of film and the birth of modern consumer culture: rising incomes, discretionary spending, increased leisure time, a rapid increase in new technologies, growth of urban areas, and women entering the workplace (Gamson, 1994). Early celebrity endorsers served merely to introduce products and recommend them to consumers. Mullan (1997) described how a review of popular magazines of the 1920s indicates a shift away from heroes to a new category of celebrities. This amplifies Daniel Boorstin's (1962/1992) widely accepted definition of celebrity—persons known for their well-known-ness.

Jamieson and Campbell (2001) suggested the following about the way media figures in advertising build associations that make their behavior worth emulating:

> When celebrities appear in commercials, they are often there to testify to the worth of a product. Sometimes they function as pseudo-authorities. What qualifies Ed McMahon as an expert on mayonnaise, motorcycles, or sunglasses? At best, celebrities speaking outside their field of achievement give testimony about their ordinary experience, experiences no more authoritative than yours and mine, about how coffee tastes or how well a detergent works. Often, the celebrity not only tells us why he or she uses the product but also hints that if we want to be like him or her, we ought to use this product. (237)

Fowles (1996) reported that entertainers receive about 60% of their income from advertising. In addition to appearing in advertisements, media figures make personal appearances, promote their own product lines, and hawk merchandise from movies in which they have appeared, among other promotional activities.

THE ILLUSION OF INTIMACY

In contemporary U.S. society, emulation provides only a partial explanation for the use of media figures in advertising. At times, advertisements, along with other media content, create the illusion of interpersonal contact when media figures speak directly out of the television and address audiences personally. Horton and Wohl (1956) defined this as a form of social interaction—"intimacy at a distance." Levy (1979) suggested that such interactions may be demonstrated by the audience's reaction to meanings attributed to a media figure. From a cultural perspective, this artificial involvement is an elementary form of social activity that Snow (1988) concludes has gained a "taken-for-granted status" (204).

Advertisements at times create the illusion of participating when spokespersons speak directly to the audience as if to address them personally. Caughey (1984) described this illusion as an important part of everyday American life in which "media consumption directly parallels actual social interaction" (37). Schickel (1985) referred to the "illusion of intimacy between the television viewer and the celebrity spokesperson" to explain how celebrities become viewers' friends (4).[1] As culture is the result of people acting through social forms, an imaginary social relationship may connect audiences to a celebrity who appears in an advertisement, a concept advanced by Caughey (1984).

P. Berger and Luckmann (1966) described this participation in "multiple realities" as a play form that helps us to make sense of reality. Gamson (1994) said:

> a good chunk of the audience reads the celebrity text in its own language, recognizing and often playing with the blurriness of its vocabulary. They leave open the question of authenticity and along with it the question of merit. For them, celebrity is not a prestige system, nor a postmodern hall of mirrors, but much as it is in the celebrity-watching tourist circuit, a game. (173)

The role that advertising plays in this process is to interrupt and then extend the game as members of an audience move from one reality, news or entertainment programming, to "supermarkets, bathrooms and bars" (Caughey, 1984: 34). This is not, however, a passive experience, but one that resembles interactions in actual social relationships. As the individual takes on the role of objectified others he or she assigns a complimentary role to the media figure that might include father figure, good citizen, or lover, among others. Although advertising may temporarily take the viewer, reader, or listener out of his or her ordinary experience, the advertisements are locked into the values, motives, and roles embedded in contemporary U.S. middle-class society. In this sense, audience members get to interact with individuals that they may hold in very high esteem in the context of their everyday lives. Although Schudson (1984) supported the notion of divine power for media figures, Caughey categorized their influence more in the realm of middle-class values. It is, to some degree, a question of idolatry versus identification. As individuals operate within these multiple realities they may for a time become the media figure; that is they may closely identify with the celebrity. The following example is of a young athlete who, for a time, is transformed into a movie character.

> There's a movie called *Rudy* about a small guy whose life goal is to be on the Notre Dame football team. Because he's small there isn't much chance of him making the team. But the guy, Rudy, perseveres and eventually gets on the team and plays. At the end of the movie where Rudy's involved in the last play of the game, you hear the fans yelling "Rudy, Rudy, Rudy." The movie is based on the real-life experiences of this guy. And, I had the same experience. When I was in high school, I was considered too small to make the football team, but I wanted to play and persevered the same way Rudy did. I totally identified with the character and when I played my friends would shout "Rudy, Rudy, Rudy." I became Rudy.

This example demonstrates how the connection to the media figure transcends media consumption. This is not uncommon as Caughey (1984) said, "Even when the TV is turned off, the book closed, or the newspaper thrown away, people continue to engage in artificial relationships with the figures they have 'met' in the media" (39).

MEDIA FIGURES AS CULTURAL REFERENTS

Schudson (1984) described how the audience viewing a media figure in an advertisement draws on other frames in which the celebrity has appeared in order to give meaning to this experience. In other words, viewers generally do not initially learn about celebrities through appearances in advertising but in some other media context or form that is part of their larger system of referents. Reeves (1987) confirmed that meanings ascribed to a media figure may come in part from knowledge gained from some other appearance. Schudson (1984) claimed that the media figure's appearance in an advertisement, which itself contributes to intertextual complexity, is "highly abstracted and self-contained" (211). Personalities have to "appear, suggesting a pulling back into well-established characters" (213). Advertising "simplifies and typifies. It does not claim to picture reality as it is but reality as it should be—life and lives worth emulating" (215). Emulation is not simply, as Veblen (1973) described it, conspicuous consumption or the subordinate trying to emulate the superordinate. The notion of emulation has grown more complicated by the diversity of American culture and the complexity of the individual's experience with commercial media. Rather than imitating the powerful, Douglas and Isherwood (1996) saw cultural consumption as a means of expression. Goods and services carry with them symbolic expression whose importance may be expressed through association with media figures. In this sense, the media figure provides a symbolic and communicative connection to the goods and services being advertised. In other words, media figures may confer value on an object within the information system of advertising.

This abstraction may be the inducement—wonder that leads to consent—for the viewer to enter into a pseudosocial interaction with a media figure appearing in an advertisement. This is a significant cultural function even if media figures only temporarily take audiences beyond their actual everyday experiences. In this sense, audiences get to interact with individuals they may hold in very high esteem even in the context of their everyday lives, which Altheide and Snow (1979) suggested may be boring when compared to the highly entertaining situations depicted within the dramatic conventions of mass media and in advertising. Boredom may provide a partial explanation why media figures appearing in advertising, as well as those appearing in entertainment and news programming, take viewers beyond actual experience. Additionally, it may be that a media figure's repeated appearances have a cumulative effect as a pseudosocial relationship develops between the media figure and the viewer or reader. The accumulation of pseudosocial experience leads to an intertextual layering through which the relationship may take on greater meaning and dimension. Caughey (1984) posited that the social world of Americans includes more media figures than actual persons.

EXPERIENCING MEDIA FIGURES

Generally, individuals describe media consumption in terms of being transported to another, sometimes disorienting, world in which they may become "involved" in the interactions of those who appear in programming and advertising. Horton and Wohl (1956) described this as creating a bond of intimacy. This experience is closely tied to the notion of suspension of disbelief in which individuals are out of touch with the actual world and in touch with their imaginary social world. Horton and Wohl reported that the fan develops loyalty to the media figure over time, as the fan sees the media figure as reliable and predictable. Reduction theory (C. Berger, 1985) similarly suggests that over time relationships develop through a process of increased certainty (C. Berger & Calabrese, 1975). Providing certainty in a relatively unstable world may be one of the more important roles media figures play in the culture. Appearance of media figures in advertising is a form of expression that as Douglas and Isherwood (1996) said, "make visible and stable the categories of the culture" (38).

Although some individuals rely on the certainty and predictability of media figures in their imaginary relationships, others indicate a more complex dimension, one that combines intimacy with a measure of skepticism. There is a natural tension within the imaginary social relationship, a dimension of which expands on Sunnafrank's (1986) conclusion that found closeness could be increased or decreased depending on the information learned. Gamson (1994) developed a typology of "celebrity-watching audiences" which he used to explain why some individuals become more involved with media figures than others. He referred to the "traditional believer" as one type of individual that "deflects reasoned evaluations . . . in favor of fantasy or personal-identification relationships" (192).

EXPLORING IMAGINARY SOCIAL RELATIONSHIPS

It may be accurate to depict, as Schudson (1984) did, a character that on the screen or page is flattened by the one-dimensional media world that turns that character into an abstraction. This abstraction, according to Schudson, limits the audience in the ways in which it connects to the media figure. Media figures may be seen as attractive, interesting, or charismatic individuals. "Credibility of the media figure may encourage individuals to believe in the quality of a product, or believe in their own inadequacy and thus develop a need for a product, or they may be reminded of their own inadequacies that may be helped by a product" (Schudson, 1984: 224). Schudson maintained that the object of a celebrity endorsement is not intended to lead to a direct influence on the purchase of a product, but rather to connect the product to the "superhuman world of the gods" (228). However, informants indicate through their descriptions of imaginary social relationships with media figures, they inflate those images—adding dimension to the interaction—as evidenced in the descriptions of their attraction to media figures.[2] Informants generally learn about or enter into these relationships through the media figure's repeated appearances in news, entertainment programming, or sports events. Repeated exposure, however, does not equate with a deep and abiding relationship as informants indicate media figures may operate on several levels ranging from early impressions—both positive and negative—to physical or social attraction that holds some potential for modeling or imitative behavior. For individuals involved in these varying degrees of relationship, media figure appearances in advertising serve a variety of functions. One basic function of their repeated appearances and subsequent exposure to the audience is the maintenance of the relationship with the media figure. Individuals also may have used the media figure's appearance in the advertisement to further explore their attraction, to question some aspect of the media figure's character or role, or to reinforce or diminish feelings toward the media figure. Therefore, the media figure's appearance in the advertisement may serve as a mediating role: to keep the relationship current and to enliven, reinforce, or alter existing attitudes toward the media figure. In this sense, the relationship with the media figure can be meaningful, but individuals can also remake or unmake meaning, variations that need to be accounted for in any meaning-making system.

Over the past decade product endorsements by media figures have become routine. McAllister (1996) pointed to the following examples from the sitcom *Seinfeld*:

> When *Seinfeld* was the hip show, advertisers rushed to use these characterizations to make the show a referent system: Julia Louis-Dreyfus redoes her Elaine characterization on commercials for Nice 'n Easy hair treatments; Jerry Seinfeld makes observations worthy of his stand-up routine on American Express commercials; Jason Alexander is a George–like character on Rold Gold Pretzel commercials, and George's parents pitch the wonders of AT&T; Michael Richards maintains his Kramer persona in Pepsi commercials. (114)

Informants know of a large number of media figures appearing in advertisements, and express familiarity with fictional characters appearing in advertisements. These fictional characters included Madge the manicurist, the Maytag repairman, Sarah Tucker, and Morris the cat, to name a few. Informants are able to cite a range of media figures they may have been introduced to through appearances in the media, for whom they have over time developed great admiration, and who appear in advertising: Gillian Anderson, Joe Namath, Fran Drescher, Bill Cosby, Joan Lunden, and Joan Rivers to name a few. The following exemplifies an informant's attraction toward Gillian Anderson:

> Gillian Anderson did this ad for Saturn cars. She plays a savvy professional who is in the market to buy a reliable new car. In the commercial every car dealer she goes to treats her like an idiot, then she goes to the Saturn dealer and is treated like an equal. By the end of the commercial she not only buys a Saturn but is now selling them, playfully showing guys the vanity mirror. I saw this ad as I was about to graduate from college, and of course I recognized Gillian Anderson from the *X-Files*. I got the idea to apply to Saturn for a job not only because I loved the product and knew a lot about it, but because Gillian Anderson did too. I respect Gillian Anderson. She is close to my age and we both have a conservative image, but possess a definite wild side. I can't say how seeing her in the commercial affected my purchase of the car, but it certainly affirmed in my mind that I was making the right decision.

A homemaker recalls her reaction toward seeing the former *Good Morning America* co-host, Joan Lunden in a commercial:

> I regard Joan Lunden as a trusted friend. I choose to watch her primarily because I like her style. When she happens to be sick or on vacation I miss her. I've suffered through her pregnancies, and when I had children of my own, I bought Beechnut baby food based on her recommendation. I don't think she's some kind of goddess whose words I have to obey, but I do think she's an intelligent, responsible person, and I respect her opinion. When she starred in *Mother's Day* on cable I watched and I suppose I'll watch her on the show *Everyday,* as well. I especially enjoyed the clip at the beginning of the program showing her going through her daily routine: waking up, getting to work, exercising, grocery shopping, etc. I suppose she does affect my behavior because she gives me confidence. She seems normal, and she has also attained goals that I value: She's a bright, attractive woman with a happy family and successful career. So if she can do it, I can too. I will stop to watch Joan Lunden in a commercial because it's like having a friend in for coffee. I trust her and enjoy seeing her and her baby. Because I like the product, I feel vindicated whenever a Beechnut commercial comes on. When the Alar scare cropped up, Beechnut reassured consumers they didn't use that pesticide—of course not—Joan wouldn't speak for a company that did.

The informant describes the relationship as safe and predictable—one that had grown over a number of years. That safety and predictability extends from the media figure's appearances in entertainment and news programming into her advertising appearances and denotes an intertextual complexity connected through the various frames in which the media figure is experienced. A college student's description of an imaginary social relationship with Bill Cosby,[3] who many Americans have grown to admire over a long period of time, also exemplifies this predictability:

> Bill Cosby is a fine example of the well-rounded celebrity. He possesses many attributes he has applied to his career. The way in which he presents himself is unique because of the way he shares himself and his personality in everything he does. I admire Bill Cosby because of his individuality. He is the ideal model for Black youth to model themselves after. I try very hard to make my own character like him. I feel that Cosby and I share that characteristic of trying to be different. Bill's personality is an important factor when it comes to his well-rounded character. There is a time and place for everything and Bill Cosby observes this. He shares humor and sincerity whenever the time or whatever the occasion. He seems to know when and when not to. He exhibits self-control. I try to exhibit this attribute and I hope to be as successful as Bill Cosby. Also, his accomplishments in the media field have been a tremendous reflection on the Black community because he's a positive character. I hope to be able to accomplish as much in my life as he has in his. What a fulfilled life of goal conquering!

Informants express an awareness of particular aspects of Bill Cosby's life, chief among them, that he holds a doctorate in education. This, they say, translates into his unique ability to deal with children in advertisements. They not only admire the media figure, they used his appearance in advertising to reinforce some generally held belief and to find significant meaning in the experience. Informants refer to Bill Cosby, and to other media figures, as people to whom they feel close. Using first names—referring to Bill Cosby as Bill, for example—implies a familiarity that parallels other imaginary experiences with media figures, primary of which are fantasies and dreams.

ENHANCING, DIMINISHING, AND MAINTAINING IMAGINARY RELATIONSHIPS

Fowles (1996) suggested that when media figures appear in advertisements they carry "certain valuable contextual inferences."

The performers have found their fame within the domain of popular culture, and when they reappear in the domain of advertising, they to one degree or another bring with themselves an aura of entertainment and diversion. When Candice Bergen testifies to the advantages of Sprint telephone service, the much enjoyed "Murphy Brown" is testifying also, when the retired Larry Bird appears in a Nike commercial, the active Larry Bird, memorable leader of the Celtics, is there too. (128-129)

The bond of intimacy that may develop through repeated media appearances would be expected to continue into the media figure's appearance in an advertisement. The appearance, however, may also serve as a meta-communicative signal (Glenn & Knapp, 1987) that may disrupt the individual's suspension of disbelief and increase uncertainty about the media figure. Self-professed fans of particular media figures appearing in advertising express an expectation that the media figure will look or act a certain way, or might appear in expected contexts. There is an expectation regarding the synergy between a spokesperson, the product, the message, the context of the advertisement, and the medium of communication. Informants point to the synergy between Frank Perdue of the Purdue Chicken Company, because "he looks like a chicken." Joan Rivers is admired because she is "straightforward," "outspoken," "blunt," or a "smart-ass." The physical resemblance of Frank Perdue to a chicken connects him to the product he promotes. Joan Rivers, as a straightforward and outspoken individual, was certainly consistent with promoting a phone service attempting to break through the advertising clutter and distinguish itself among the competition and certainly these attributes contribute to her success selling products via the Home Shopping Network. Candice Bergen played the same sarcastic role of Murphy Brown when she was spokesperson for Sprint. And, Sprint's current spokesperson, Sela Ward, displays the same independent mindedness in their advertisements, as does her character on the television series *Once and Again*.

Inconsistency among these variables of celebrity character, product, message, and medium serves as a signal that something is not quite right. Fowles (1996) said "Endorsements succeed only when consumers feel that meanings can shift along unimpeded paths from performer to product—either because of an inherent affinity between the two or because of the ingenuity of the agency's creative team, or both" (131). Strong identification with the celebrity is not enough for consumers to positively evaluate a product or its usefulness to them. As one informant reported:

My relationship with Joe Namath goes back to his legendary status with my favorite football team, the New York Jets. During his career

> he was able to go beyond the status of star regional athlete to enter the realm of the national folk hero. He did this by combining traditional football talent with a unique personality and sense of style that seemed to reflect the new nonconformist mood of the country.

This individual suggests that Namath "cashed in" by selling everything from men's cologne to pantyhose. Of his appearance in a Nike shoe advertisement he says:

> I don't know if I feel betrayed in any way, but part of the shine has certainly come off of one of my heroes whose actions and statements are now compromised by the lure of financial gain. By opening himself up to the highest bidder I feel that Joe Namath is no longer "free" to express the individualism that first attracted me to him.

Some advertisers apparently understand this interaction and in some instances use antagonism to gain viewers' attention. Informants point to the following examples: John McEnroe, the "bad boy of tennis," and Larry Hagman, who played J.R. Ewing on *Dallas*. In instances where these two media figures have appeared in advertisements, the advertiser uses the inverse of the stereotypical fan relationship to gain attention. One informant describes Fran Dresher, who appeared in the television program *The Nanny*, as "someone possessing all of the traits I try to avoid in a friend."

> She is everything that I am not. She annoys me. Her voice sends a jolt through my spine that has me quickly reaching for the omnipotent remote control. She reminds me of my nosy neighbor and one of my college roommates. When I see her in a commercial, I am briefly transported to the days in college when I lived in a house with five other women—a bittersweet remembrance. This experience is both pleasurable and an irritation.

The Jenny Craig Company selected Monica Lewinsky, fresh from the Clinton scandal, as their spokesperson hoping to take advantage of her notoriety. "Some Jenny Craig franchises refused to pay for the ads. 'As a person who has been successful on our program, she'd done great,' said a franchise owner. 'But as a person to look up to, there are certainly some issues there. . . . I wouldn't be pleased if my daughter came home and said 'I want to be just like Monica Lewinsky'" (cited in Jamieson & Campbell, 2001: 238). Inversion has the potential to attract attention, but the advertisement also can repel those for whom the inversion is transparent.

If predictability were simple to construct and maintain, advertisers would certainly take advantage of such ritualized encounters (Sunnafrank, 1986). However, because imaginary social relationships are dynamic, the nature of such encounters—the advertisement as the point of interaction—may be beyond the advertiser's control. In the following instance, a young man reported losing, then regaining, respect for Bill Cosby when he chose not to appear in an advertisement.

> I think the way Bill Cosby was doing Coke commercials was misleading. I think I read in a magazine that he really didn't like the new Coke or drink the new Coke. Now that I don't see him doing any more commercials for Coke, I can respect him more and I would be more likely to buy a product he endorsed, if I was interested in the product.

A re-evaluation that the media figure has not sold out reinforces that he or she has integrity and allows the relationship to remain in its predictable mold.

Sometimes informants report extreme emotional reactions such as being "horrified" or watching "in disbelief" when they have seen a media figure appear in an advertisement; something is askew regarding their personal expectations for a media figure. This negative appraisal may, for a time, causes audiences to pay closer attention to the advertisement, or at least part of the message as they question something about the media figure, like the appropriateness of the appearance in an advertisement. Over a short period of time not believing that Bill Cosby likes Coke, for example, may create tension in the relationship. This tension may build over repeated exposure to the advertisement as evidenced by several informants' highly emotional reactions to these instances.

If the relationship is important, individuals may attempt to reconcile the conflicts that emerge between all of these elements. This is evidenced in the earlier description of the reaction to Bill Cosby choosing not to appear in Coke commercials. The tension between what is expected of the media figure and the media figure's "unexpected" behavior is important to advertisers attempting to get the audience's attention and may be emotionally unsettling for audiences involved in long-term imaginary relationships. For example, one Gen-Xer recalls the positive impact Orson Welles had on his life prior to his appearance in a wine advertisement:

> Orson Welles demonstrated his independence from mainstream ideas and showed a willingness to suffer the consequences of pursuing his own course, traits that I have tried to develop within myself through the inspiration of figures like Welles. His emphasis on quali-

ty at the expense of acclaim led him to be a rather obscure figure for much of his professional career. . . . It has led me to develop some-what of a maverick attitude toward society, resulting in my taking unpopular stands on issues, both social and professional ones. While this has sometimes gotten me into trouble, I hope it has also earned me the same kind of grudging respect frequently accorded Welles.

The informant, having recalled seeing Welles in a wine advertisement, describes this re-evaluation of the actor as "seriously disillusioning." He says he felt cheated: "It was not a happy experience." Even though some individuals show great admiration for a media figure, they remain suspicious of advertising's motives. C. Berger and Calabrese (1975) maintained that attraction should increase through repeated exposure. When audiences, however, are very familiar with a media figure, through repeated appearances in news, sports, or entertainment pro-gramming, they may react quite negatively to that media figure's appearance in an advertisement. A young woman's reaction to Linda Ellerbee's appearance in a Maxwell House coffee advertisement serves as a case in point:

I believe part of my attraction to news is that as a major link between me and the world. It has been a vehicle that has released powerful personal emotions. It has brought stories of events that have gen-uinely shocked me, saddened me, stopped me in my tracks. The fact that Linda Ellerbee did a Maxwell House coffee commercial offends my sensibilities. How dare someone use the mantle of jour-nalistic respectability to promote a single product. Somehow the fact that she was involved in news programming makes her more respectable and objective in your eyes, which makes her promotion of a product seem narrow, limited, money-grubbing, and objection-able. Since I've never had any cause to take Willard Scott [the weather reporter] seriously, I just see him as another media figure turning a quick buck.

One homemaker reported that she cannot accept the inconsistency between the "bad guy" role an actor portrays on a soap opera and his "good guy" role in a television commercial:

I remember that guy who plays Tad Martin, a playboy on *All My Children*, doing a commercial for Woolite. I couldn't believe it. I said, what's a dog like him doing in a commercial for a product that is sup-posed to be gentle and soft? It made me hate him more.

Informants' descriptions of this inconsistency suggest a range of poten-tial reactions. The immediate result of this inconsistency is the expression of disbelief in the advertisement's message and questioning of their feelings about the media figure. The individuals might also have questioned how this new role would impact the media figure's career, and therefore the relationship.

Till and Shimp (1998) used an associative memory framework to study transfer of feelings from media figure to audience. Although the advertiser expects there to be a transfer of positive feelings toward the product endorser to the brand, they found a correlation between negative feelings toward the product endorser and lower evaluations of the brand. Even if predictability and certainty resulted from past experience with the media figure, informants maintain that this had little to do with the media figure's authority to make product claims or to proclaim product virtues. As one woman succinctly put it, "who can be an authority on Coke? If you drink it, you're an authority." The individual added:

> That Pizza Hut commercial where those celebrities just sit up there and eat pizza. I don't care who it is . . . the noises they are making . . . I'm ready to go eat. . . . It's only because I've been to Pizza Hut that things are already established for me that make it easy to make the decision.

Audiences may initially be drawn to an advertisement for its entertainment value, or because of values with which they identify. The message, however, may be rejected in some fashion as the initial attraction is counterbalanced by the media figure's perceived expertise or authority. Questioning the media figure's authority to make product claims is an important aspect of the imaginary social interaction. An elementary school teacher states in reaction to a media figure's appearance in an office copier commercial: "What does he [the celebrity] know about copiers?" A homemaker says: "And what about that yogurt commercial with all those celebrities speaking French. . . . What's that guy's name? . . . who you know has never eaten yogurt in his life!" Individuals who could not provide a rationale for the media figure's authority may have used existing beliefs about the media figure to question the product and some aspects of the relationship. This kind of skepticism appears to help individuals to distance themselves from the perceived power of advertising (and media figures who appear in advertisements) to persuade. This questioning is an important matter for audiences and may play a larger cultural role. As such the media figure's appearance may serve as a warning, signaling audiences to be wary of what is to follow. Individuals express a desire to separate the celebrity from the sales pitch. Other qualities or attributes—social or physical—of the media figure appear to be significant to audiences in getting and maintaining their attention. In cases where the media figure appears to have authority the individual does not perceive the media figure to possess, the individual may reject at least part of the message. This situation holds the potential for re-evaluation of the relationship.

AUDIENCE AWARENESS OF THE CELEBRITY SYSTEM

Individuals display an astute awareness of the "system" in which media figures operate, and they use advertising appearances in a dialectical manner in order to adjust their knowledge and beliefs about media figures. Appearances in advertising, therefore, become part of the explanation process in which audiences understand what is going on in a media figure's life. Informants report varying, often contradictory, reasons why media figures appear in advertisements. These reasons are similar to those reported in the literature—money, exposure, and versatility.

Individuals say a media figure's appearance in an advertisement at the same time that an actor is performing in a current entertainment program serves as a signal, perhaps indicating that she or he was about to leave the series. A college student provided the following example:

> Like Nina who left *All My Children* and started doing Neet commercials. Maybe nothing is going on with their character at the time, so they do commercials if they are getting ready to leave the show—appearing in advertisements—their managers can show that the actor can be versatile. Maybe he's a playboy on the soap but he can act sentimental in some other role. Maybe appearing in the commercial will lead to another role.

A homemaker explains her understanding of the reasons why some actors appear in advertisements and others do not:

> The majority of older actors don't do commercials, except for comediennes. For many actors who have been at it so long, it's not dignified enough to do commercials. Others will do commercials for charities, like Bob Hope. He did do commercials for Gulf, Exxon . . . or is it Texaco? Maybe he was just been doing them for years and thinks that's just part of his role. I would say that older actors don't do them and younger actors do, because the younger ones are at the bottom of the ladder and have to gain respect.

Whether accurate or not, this general perception suggests audiences may use the appearance to further understand the media system in which advertising operates. A college student says, "If you are already established and you appear in an advertisement, it may mean that everything is not right in your career. Advertising is a place on the entertainment ladder to work your way up from." McAllister (1996) echoed this when he said, "Advertisers love to use motion picture celebrities as referent systems. Movie stars know, however, that appearing in commercials dilutes their star quality. When you see a movie star shilling for a product, the glamour and allure of the star decreases" (57). Other informants say advertising is the place celebrities begin the long road down. And yet others conclude that advertising is just a stopping off place—a place to wait for good roles. Therefore, there is little inherent significance regarding Jane (Josie Bissett) from television's *Melrose Place* appearing in advertisements for an underarm deodorant or make-up. What is of significance is what audiences do with the appearance as a part of their imaginary social interaction. The appearance may become fodder for gossip—grist for the mill, but it also might play a more significant role in helping individuals to make sense of their world. As further evidence, a homemaker speaks about her understanding of the system in the following description:

> The system is not set up for the celebrity to step forward and say, "I want to do this because I believe in the product." It's oriented toward the business side where they will say, "Let's get so-and-so to do this commercial because it will work."

Perspectives may vary somewhat as to why a media figure appears in an advertisement, but rationalizing the appearance is an important interaction in the imaginary social relationship. Individuals also use such appearances to make value judgments about the capitalist system. As one middle-aged man put it, "I don't see how it (appearing in advertisements) could be deceitful. It's acting. It's a job." The informant adds, "Actors appearing in commercials may be seen by producers and obtain other acting jobs, making the process totally acceptable." Some informants also acknowledge that some celebrities will not do commercials because "it's beneath them . . . they don't believe in the product or they don't need the money. Some do have morals and standards and won't budge. . . . Money doesn't affect them."

Individuals use media figures to make moral judgments about society. The general notions that "it's okay to make lots of money doing small tasks" (advertisements), that a certain level of "deceit is acceptable," and that "we (individuals) are responsible for being able to discern the truth from lies" were reinforced through appearances of media figures in advertisements. "If the celebrity had no connection to the product and doesn't use it—that's not deceitful," one informant says. "She's just trying to make money." Media figures appearances in advertising, therefore, are far from taken as "art for art's sake." The meaning ascribed to these appearances suggests the audience is wary. This is further evidence that the aesthetic level is only one level on which audiences approach the appearance of media figures in advertising.

CONCLUSION

If advertising is relatively timeless and placeless, as Schudson (1984) suggested, audiences may ground their experience of the advertisement in an imaginary social relationship. Such pseudo relationships serve as compensation for experience that the audience otherwise cannot have. Part of the meaning comes through the predictability of a media figure's repeated appearances in advertisements. The path toward the social construction of reality, at least as far as media figures appearing in advertising, is not a straightforward or simple one. Some individuals demonstrate a strong attraction to and unyielding faith in certain media figures. Other individuals, who displayed a long-term attraction, sometimes express an uncertainty about the media figure's appearance in advertisements. This skepticism does not necessarily affect feelings for a media figure, as the individual may seek a rationale as to why the media figure appeared in an advertisement. Product purveyors have grown somewhat skeptical of the use of media figures as endorsers. Public embarrassment, exemplified in the case of O. J. Simpson (indicted and later acquitted on charges of murder), resulted in a liability for the brand. This has resulted in the trend toward using deceased celebrities who are scandal proof (Goldman, 1994).

Paralleling relationships in real life, audiences can balance positive feelings for media figures with negative or neutral attitudes towards their appearances in advertisements. Furthermore, the advertiser's attempt to associate a media figure with a product may serve as a meta-communicative signal that, while gaining audience attention, may also hold the potential to increase uncertainty. The connections between product and media figure, therefore, are part of the complex dimension of experience. The aesthetic connection is just one factor audiences use to evaluate the media figure's performance or appearance in an advertisement, and in the broader sense to make judgments about advertising and the capitalist system.

Schudson (1984) concluded, "consumers in front of a television screen are relatively unwary" (227). This is what allows, he suggests, the advertisement to be successful. However, even if the media figure's appearance in the advertisement is flattened, viewers make up the difference—fill in the gap—through their pseudosocial interactions.

Repeated appearances across programming create an intertextual web that can be likened to the complex system of actual social relationships. The advertisement itself is a means by which audiences can "reach out and touch someone" to form relationships, alter existing relationships, and, perhaps end relationships. Advertising, which is hardly neutral territory, is a point at which many media experiences converge. The confluence of information, gossip, and past media experiences sometimes come together at this juncture to provide meaning to the viewer involved in an imaginary social relationship. Gamson (1994) supported this conclusion when he said:

> Playing with culture offers participants the chance to work through in a free realm everyday life experiences that typically appear in arenas of consequence. Celebrities are particularly suited to these games precisely because they are encoded in a semifictional language: audiences can easily play evaluation and judgment games "as if" with real people but without an ultimate authority [gossip], or they can play at the borders between real and not real [detectives]. (185)

In a sense, audiences' actual social situations are interconnected to multiple realities; advertising is just one of them. Enculturation into this imaginary social interaction begins at an early age (James & McCain, 1982; Reid & Frazer, 1980). Appearances by media figures in advertising are just one form in our mass mediated culture where audiences participate in the give and take with a multitude of media figures. Attracted to some of these media figures, audiences incorporate them into their imaginary social worlds.

ENDNOTES

1. An informant wondered why his daughter always played close to the glow of the television screen. He reported that she only paid attention to what was going on when the commercials came on. After observing her, the informant became aware that she was paying attention because unlike dramatic programming, the people in the commercials were talking directly to her.
2. See the Appendix for an explanation of the ethnographic method utilized to collect and interpret the imaginary social relationships described in this chapter.
3. Bill Cosby was a spokesperson for Jello for 27 years.

6

SOCIAL DISCOURSE AND ADVERTISING AS A SOCIAL PRACTICE

The richness of language plays an important part in everyday life, and this is no less so for advertising. Language, as Fairclough (1989) stated, is a socially conditioned process through which individuals may internalize what is socially produced and made available to them for later use. The use of advertising, like the socially conditioned process of language, is a social practice within the context of ordinary American life. Meyers (1994) maintained that everyday talk is different than institutionalized talk like that of advertising. "Everyday life is not institutional—not politics, or church services, or courts . . . talk in everyday life is man to man, or woman to woman, or woman to man or whatever" (108). Everyday talk, Meyers said, stands in contrast to advertising talk. However, as Fairclough (1989) countered, "there is not an external relationship between language and society, but an internal and dialectical relationship" (23). The language of advertising provides a vocabulary that serves as a means of self-expression that helps position individuals socially (Ewen, 1988).

The advertising industry may measure the success or failure of a campaign by its ability to infiltrate everyday conversation.

To be called "great," advertising should do something more; it must get talked about. It must be so unique that it becomes a topic of conversation, not just at the agency and the client, but among members of the sales force, the trade, the competition and the general public.

It must be so audacious that it gets written about in the newspapers, discussed in supermarkets, worried about in boardrooms or even joked about on talk shows. (Cornish, 1987: 64)

It is this very institutionalized talk that circulates through everyday life that advertisers seek. The principle behind the industry's position is that if one can control the "talk," one can to some degree control the marketplace. The circulation of institutionalized talk, like the vocabulary of advertising, may be based on the idea of coercion, but it operates on the level of consent. There is more to the process than creating a great advertisement and assuming that it will become water cooler talk.

This chapter is concerned with the way the language of advertising circulates in everyday American life, a social practice in which individuals utilize its content as self-expression and utilize it as a means to socially position themselves. The chapter describes individuals' use of the content of advertising in their everyday conversations and the ways in which catch phrases and slogans, along with other elements of advertising, circulate through the culture. It also describes the contribution of the media to the process as, for example, when a character in a movie uses the content of an advertisement within a dramatic scene. The chapter suggests that advertising use is a play form that is rich in complexity and sophisticated in application.

Advertisers are interested in consumers' acquisition of advertising language—phrases, slogans and other elements—only to the extent that its popularity is associated with the promotion of the sale of a product or service. Advertisements that "get talked about" have a common denominator, "that of being different from the mainstream, from the status quo. In the process, they surprise. They may even shock. And, for many, they make life all the more interesting as a result" (Marra, 1990: 41). Meyers (1994) referred to a British advertising campaign for Nescafe. He said that what makes the advertisement "remarkable" is the "way people talk about it" (117). The campaign seems to have taken on a life of its own as it showed up in newspaper headlines. Meyers claimed that what may be learned from advertising is similar to that of other media and other institutions, like the church. "It is not a natural realm," he said, "but one shaped by the way we talk about it. Ads are part of that talk" (117). And from a cultural point of view, advertisers are interested in social discourse regarding their products when "word of mouth" supports sales. Gillespie's (1995) fieldwork supports this position:

One of the most tangible examples of the way that the discourses of TV and everyday life are intermeshed is when jingles, catch phrases and humorous storylines of favorite ads are incorporated into everyday speech. Ads provide a set of shared cultural reference points, images and metaphors that spice local speech. (178)

Gillespie, who studied teenagers in Southall England, said that her informants understand the persuasive and informational qualities of advertising, and also appreciate advertising as an entertainment form. She described informants' appreciation of advertising as "recompense for their lack of consumer power" (178).

Advertisers may attempt to control the infiltration of language into social discourse, but there is no evidence to support the predictability of this phenomenon. Therefore, it does not matter how much strategic information an advertiser acquires in an effort to know and understand the target audience; some aspects of the consumer's appropriation of advertising are clearly unpredictable and uncontrollable. Furthermore, the economic value of advertising-based language is only part of the equation as advertising operates in the social and cultural economy as well.

APPROPRIATION OF ADVERTISING CONTENT

Advertisers construct meaning in order to communicate quickly, almost instantaneously. And, many advertisements rely on symbols with which consumers are already highly familiar—items, scenes, and relationships from everyday lives (Goffman, 1976). Advertisements are highly structured, tending to be one or two pages in magazines, 60 seconds on the radio, and 30 or perhaps 15 seconds on television. Because of their form, format, and structure, advertisements are unique among media content. In a fast-paced U.S. society and because of rising media costs, it has become increasingly necessary for advertisers to communicate in an expedient manner using short cuts to language such as slang phrases. Advertising lends itself well to these financial and cultural needs. Fracturing the form (e.g., the Energizer battery advertisement in which the rabbit repeatedly enters from what appears to be another commercial) is another means by which advertisers capture attention. Advertising language, more so than any other institutionalized form of communication, is constructed for this very purpose—to communicate quickly and efficiently. The fast pace of U.S. society extends beyond the speed at which media communicates to the ways in which individuals find ways to expediently communicate with one another. Americans, by and large, have over time learned to use the contents of advertisements automatically, utilizing some advertising content in the context of social discourse. This education is ongoing beginning in childhood with early experiences with mass media

(James & McCain, 1982). Mick (1987) amplified this point in his discussion of advertising story grammars, a rule-based system that eases our understanding of advertising.

Individuals appropriate advertising's content for various social and cultural reasons, and the process of appropriation is quite complex. This is a part of the advertising process that goes beyond economic importance, and extends into social and cultural significance. When individuals appropriate the content of advertising, a play form develops where they may use an advertising element in the context of a conversation to emphasize a specific point, for example, and simultaneously demonstrate their connection to mass media content. There is a social reward not only for "scoring a point" in a conversation, but also for showing off one's media savvy.

This demonstration of media knowledge is one of the requirements for "membership" in American culture (Caughey, 1984). Caughey asserted that knowledge of the cultural language is necessary to fit in, but the lack of such knowledge may not automatically lead to ostracism. Movies, television, and other mass media forms, like advertising, play the role of social integrator. The mass media experience, generally, is "a means of social integration which signals that the individual is not too deviant in cultural activities" (Jowett & Linton, 1980: 83). Seeing the latest movies, for example, and being able to talk about them may be a minor form of prestige. Such media-based conversations are an "absolute guarantee of admittance to conversation with others" (83). Knowing the content of advertisements and transforming this content for appropriate use in conversations is something that is learned, something to which individuals are enculturated.

Over the years through media consumption, individuals acquire a storehouse of advertising references, catch phrases, or slogans, and they refine their ability to call these up for use in social discourse. In the context of social relationships, the use of advertising creates a common ground in which subgroups—those in the know—can declare their connectedness through the use of advertising content. The paradox is that in the process of promoting social conformity by using highly codified language, the individual also uses this content and play form as an expression of his or her individuality. Rather than "playing for no gain," the individual uses advertising to shift the equilibrium in social relationships. Sometimes these uses can bring prestige, and sometimes they can bring people closer together. Other times they can be used to help the individual maintain social distance. In this way, the individual uses particular language to assist in controlling the social situation and social relationship.

Allen (1982) noted that in everyday life, advertising catch phrases, slogans, and jingles—as well as news and entertainment programming—show up in conversations as "gregarious chatter and patter" (107). Advertising, along with other media content, may evoke instant and common responses; nothing more needs to be said.

> Media popularize and coin slang and neologisms that quickly pass into the language. Media similarly create catch phrases, buzzwords and provide reference points for simile and metaphor in everyday language. Media symbols, for example, enter the reasoning process and allow people in conversation to draw quick parallels between situations without analysis by calling up a well known symbol to connote the parallel role of a less known personality in another situation. (108)

In that process, "A ginger cat in Kansas becomes the 'Morris' [the infamous cat in the Nine Lives cat food advertisement] of the kitchen floor" (108). Allen pointed out that, "Television commercials and magazine advertising are produced to be entertaining in order to elicit attention and may be used more for amusement than simply as a source, however, unwilling or unwitting, of consumer information" (107). Allen said, "The inherent effects of the mass communications process per se are neither consensus nor conflict producing, but depend on the content and use of that content by audiences. The exchange of media content can either initiate or disrupt, sustain or weaken, damage or repair social relations" (109).

ADVERTISING USE AS PLAY

Social discourse that is associated with the use of advertising content takes the form of verbal play. Like other forms of play, advertising play as displayed in social discourse varies in creativity or inventiveness depending on many factors. Regardless of the individual's background or the social context, the meaning of this play form goes beyond the obvious desire to simply entertain, as there is greater meaning to this activity. Important to this process is that advertising messages are so malleable that individuals twist and turn them, somewhat like improvisational jazz, to fit a particular situation or relationship. Ironically, with so many advertising messages available from our cultural storehouse, only a few slogans, catch phrases, or other advertising references become a part of the common language. Once the reference does come into common use, however, it may not be as short-lived as some advertising campaigns.

Advertising language is a commodity whose value is based not only on economics, but also on its value to socially empower the individual. It is just one element in the mass media marketplace, which might include references to television sitcoms, dramas, the news, and movies, among media fare from which to choose. In the process of acquiring advertising content, we select some of these "products"—a catch phrase, for example—and adopt and adapt some of its content for use in everyday life. Paradoxically, advertisers can to some degree control what consumers will appropriate, but not when or where they will use it. And the fact that consumers use it at all, making advertising content a common feature of social discourse, is evidence that advertising contributes to stability and continuity of the culture.

In order to understand the use of advertising in the context of everyday life, Schudson (1984) suggested the need to recognize the game advertising plays with us, and the game we play with it. What kind of games do consumers play with advertising? *Playing* with the content of advertising in the context of social discourse is a phenomenon not clearly understood by advertisers, and one for which there is little empirical evidence. Play is conceptualized as free time used for largely unproductive and potentially self–satisfying activities (Stephenson, 1967). Inherent in the notion of play is the premise that much of everyday life is boring when compared to the highly entertaining situations depicted within the dramatic conventions of mass media. With regard to advertising play, the concern is not with games of fantasy or role-playing, but rather with language play; that is, with verbal expressions derived from advertisements and used in interpersonal situations. This language play, then, is like life imitating art, a kind of meta-communication in which the content of advertising becomes the content of social discourse. The use of advertising in social discourse, simply put, may make life more interesting.

Pacanowsky and Anderson (1982) provided the following playful use of advertising by policemen who referred to one another with nicknames from the media:

> Mike is a very proper young officer who uses his seat belt and neither smokes nor drinks nor swears. He is called "Mikey" after the young boy in the Life cereal commercial, but he is so named not simply because of his youthful innocence. Rather, whenever a Valley View cop sees or picks up a sleazy woman—drunk, whacked out on drugs or hustling tricks—someone will say, "Give her to Mikey, he'll eat anything." And thus, by an implication of oral sex, the wholesomeness of breakfast cereal is transformed into the unwholesomeness of sleazy women, and a comment is made on police reality and the seamy side of life. (747)

Lull (1980) investigated the uses of television in social settings, primarily during viewing, and children's play with television content has received some attention (see, e.g., James & McCain, 1982; Reid & Frazer, 1980).

Observations of advertising talk reveal that individuals develop, through the use of advertising, a high level of skill in maintaining the social structure, or in making sense of the world. The development of this skill, getting along with others, is not dissimilar to playing by the "rules of a game" (Rotzoll et al., 1976). Advertising can foster sociability, a kind of play form, by promoting participation or shared interaction, but it does so without specific purpose. In using the content of advertising in the context of social discourse, participants are "playing for no gain," and are unaware of this play (Stephenson, 1967). Stephenson referred to this as the "art of being conversational for reasons of sociability." The playfulness is illustrated in the following example. The informant's use of a well-known catch phrase eases the way to a social introduction.

> My girlfriend and I were at Howard University when she introduced her friend Carl to me. She said, "meet Mikey." I replied, "I thought his name was Carl?" She said, "Well, yes it is . . . we just call him Mikey because he eats anything."

TRANSFORMING THE CONTENT OF ADVERTISING

As the preceding example demonstrates, individuals do not use the content of an advertisement as it is given, as catch phrases and other elements are invariably transformed for use in social discourse. And although the use of advertising appears as part of the taken-for-grantedness of everyday life where consumers have little awareness of it and place little importance in it, transforming advertising content into social or political commentary may not be as simple as it appears. The process of transforming the relatively straightforward content of an advertisement is rather complex. A single transformation strategy involves at least four nearly simultaneous steps. First, there must be perception or awareness that the context is right for such use. Second, there must be an understanding of the "audience" and the social situation that would make the use meaningful. Third, the individual must draw on his or her memory to recall the phrase. And, fourth, the individual must transform the phrase from its advertising context for purposeful use in a new social context. All of this appears to take place in an instant.[1]

This process is like playing by the rules of a game, except as Goffman (1976) suggested, the rules of the game are in constant flux. Furthermore, some players are better at it than others. The transformation of the catch phrase from the Energizer battery campaign provides an illustration: In reporting on a new drug, Tolomerace, an ABC news report says, "one way to think about Tolomerace is like the Energizer Bunny. It keeps going and going." *The Wall Street Journal*, reporting on the 2000 Democratic National Convention, referred to President Bill Clinton's speech as reminiscent of "the Energizer Bunny, the little pink rabbit with the drum who keeps going and going and going." *Investors Business Daily* reports in a story about EMC Corporation that the company has the Energizer Bunny as its corporate mascot. "It just keeps going and going and going," EMC's chief executive said. And in the movie *City Slickers II*, Billy Crystal, speaking to his wife about a planned romantic evening says, "Tonight, I'm the Energizer Bunny."

These brief examples suggest that the same catch phrase can be twisted and turned, in other words played with, to suit a particular use and to fit a particular context. The given meaning gives way to the ironic meaning implied in the use; all can play with this content, not just the audience segment targeted by the advertiser. It is clear that the professional newscasters and reporter can use the phrase to gain prominence for the story, and a master comedian can incorporate the advertising reference into a movie script in an effort to connect with the audience. In other examples, ordinary people in their everyday lives transform the same phrase—it keeps going and going—for entirely different purposes.

REINTEGRATING THE CONTENT OF ADVERTISEMENTS

As a social practice, individuals use select advertisements recalled from their store of knowledge in the context of social discourse. Meaning is derived by the individual's own interpretation of the advertising content. Therefore, it is not the overt or the intended meaning of an advertising reference that is important, but the interpretation or reintegration and use of that meaning. In this sense, the bunny that keeps going and going is jettisoned from the Energizer batteries to which it was originally tethered. The function is closely related to Eco's (1979) notion of *overcoding*; complicating an already existing code by adding a circumstantial selection.

An example of this use of advertising content can be seen in the now classic catch phrase "Where's the Beef?" from a 1984 Wendy's restaurant television commercial. For a time, the phrase seemed to permeate U.S. society. At the time of the commercial's first appearance, the Gray Panthers, a rights group for the elderly, used the phrase and referenced the commercial's primary character to criticize mass media's stereotyping of the elderly. Children used the phrase "Where's the Beef?" to joke with friends, entertain parents, or to show cultural awareness. Journalists used the phrase as social commentary, in some instances humorously, to create immediate understanding in a limited amount of space (e.g., the lead paragraph of the newspaper column). And then presidential candidate Walter Mondale was able to cut across cultural boundaries, creating an immediate connection with his broad audience, when he asked, "Where's the Beef?" in Senator Gary Hart's ideas. More recently, when McDonald's admitted to seasoning its French fries with beef flavoring, a newspaper headline read, "Where's the Beef? It's in Your French Fries."

As the example illustrates, meaning appropriated from the advertisement is highly individualistic. The variety and range of message patterns exemplified in the Wendy's restaurant catch phrase while in play suggest that patterns change. "We may think of play as variations on a theme, an improvisational jazz created from message sequences" (Glenn & Knapp, 1987: 63). This variation suggests that play is a social form that connects not only to actual experience, but also to imaginary experience. The improvisational nature of play is rooted in the multiple realities in which individuals operate and serves as a mechanism for making sense of the world around us, including the messages presented in advertisments. This leads to an understanding that advertising communication is based on an information system or ecosystem in which meaning is derived through the give and take of social discourse.

Learning is not necessarily media-based, that is to say, one does not have to see a particular advertisement in order to learn how to use its catch phrase, slogan, or other element in social discourse. Phrases and jingles may be learned through repeated interaction with others indicating there is a socialization process at work. As one informant recalled, "I am not a TV watcher, but when 'Where's the beef?'" entered the social discourse, I got it, because other people were using it." The social discourse of our times is perhaps more seamless when considering interpersonal communication and mass communication; one need not necessarily attend to the advertising communication in order to learn and understand it for later use as a part of social discourse. This same phenomenon was documented during a discussion with parents after observing children in a day-care center. Parents who did not allow their children to watch television at home recalled their children's ability to play with the language of advertising. In other words, whether these children ate at McDonalds or not, they were fully immersed in the culture of McDonalds. This use not only confirms the findings of James and McCain (1982), it reaffirms that the media are not the only source of advertising content. This should not be mistaken for simple word-of-mouth advertising, as the product becomes jettisoned from the use of the catchy line or reference.

Cultural connectedness is fulfilled by seeking information that is relevant to consumers' values and meets their needs. Like jokes, over a lifetime the individual learns new catch phrases and discards older ones, although the informants provided evidence suggesting that they hold on to some advertising content for 2 to 3 years, and in some instances for 20 or more years. For example, one informant used the phrase from a 40-year-old Pepsodent toothpaste advertisement—"You'll wonder where the yellow went when you brush your teeth with Pepsodent"—as a way of describing the yellowish color of his dog. Another used a catch phrase from a vintage tire advertisement, "Where the rubber meets the road" in order to emphasize the need to "get down to business."

SOCIAL RELATIONSHIPS AND ADVERTISING USE

Advertising content offers a language through which people may speak and its use fosters their mutual socialization. The purpose of playful conversation, Stephenson (1967) suggested, is to normalize manners, to suggest certain standards of conduct, to provide leisure, and to make life easier. Sherry (1987) extended this point when he described advertising as the most potent agency of cultural stability. For example, in a very practical sense, the catch–phrase from a mouthwash advertisement becomes a useful tool to tell someone playfully, without hurting their feelings, she or he has bad breath. During a conversation an individual can say something about someone's personal hygiene, for example, without creating a hostile situation, unless that is the intent (which it sometimes is). Because the use is playful and the content is from advertising, participants understand such uses as a means to temper potentially awkward situations. Humorous transformations are illustrated in the following examples:

> In my dance class there are about 20 women. On a very hot day in the middle of a lesson, when everyone was really sweaty, the instructor said to us, "Aren't you glad you use Dial?" And the class replied in unison, "Don't you wish everybody did?"

> I regularly try to get Stephanie to laugh at my sometimes less than funny jokes. The other day I was quizzing her for an upcoming Kineseology exam. I would read the location of a particular muscle and she would respond with the name of the muscle and the action. We had already gone through several muscles when she responded to a description of the Deltoids. I quickly saw this as an opportunity to assert my "humor" saying, "Your Deltoids are ready when you are" [from a parody of a Delta Airline advertisement]. We chuckled and, yes, she made some disparaging comment about my sense of humor.

> Working in a cafeteria kitchen becomes funny after a while, especially when the cooks begin to talk about each other. Just as I was about to enter the kitchen one day, I heard several people laughing very loud. As I went in, the cook's helper came over to me and said Ernie said Mr. Gable's chicken wings look like Frank Perdue chicken wings, and Betty said, "yeah, it takes a tough man to cook a tough chicken."

The uses of advertising content takes place largely in the context of everyday face-to-face interaction and may play a role in "sustaining and weakening the more loosely woven fabric of modern social life" (Allen, 1982: 106). The notions of sustaining and weakening connote volatility in social relationships. The uses of advertising, therefore, may work to promote social distancing or closeness and it may work to strengthen or weaken relationships. In one example where two people are being introduced to one another the use of an advertising catch phrase helps break the ice.

> Last Tuesday after choir practice Don, a friend of mine, and I were introducing ourselves to some of the new ladies who had joined. We met one whose name is Charmone. So, I responded to our introduction by saying, "Don't squeeze the Charmone."

The informant reported that everyone laughed, making a potentially awkward situation humorous. The use of advertising content in some cases brings people together in laughter, particularly when the situation appears to be awkward as in the following example:

> My family, aware of my weight problem, would always get on my case about eating any kind of elaborate desserts. Sometimes the rest of the family would have cake and ice cream and when it came to me they would ask if I wanted fruit or something like that. I would get really upset and it would start some kind of argument. So when I was over at my grandparents' house, as soon as dinner was over, my grandmother would bring out Jello. And I would look at it disgustingly, because I knew that everyone else was giving up their dessert for me. So my grandfather would always say that everybody was too full for dessert anyway and he would add that even though everybody was full, "there's always room for Jello." It would lighten things up.

In situations where normalized manners are important as in a class or sitting around a dinner table, participants are more likely to engage in this play form. As Glenn and Knapp (1987) suggested, individuals are likely to go along with the game as backing out could present the individual potential problems under certain circumstances. Another informant presented a situation in which she understood how important it was to treat her auto mechanic with deference. She was able to use a catch phrase from a muffler advertisement in order to express her frustration at the mechanic's work. Her use of the content of advertising allows her to get her point across, but without being direct in expressing her feelings of frustration.

> I went to the auto repair shop the other day because my car was having starting problems. I was talking with the mechanic about the problem I was having with my car. The mechanic said he would take it for a test ride and check out the starter. When he finished he said he couldn't find any problem with the starter. I continued to press the fact by complaining further that, "I want the car to start the first time, every time."

ADVERTISING CONTENT AS SOCIAL INTEGRATOR

In order to fit into various groups, knowledge of the "home" language is necessary. The content of advertisements provide some of those common referents, thus providing common ground in social discourse. One individual described this scene during a camping trip:

> About 30 of us were split into two groups and sitting around drinking beer. At one point, as the beer drinking continued, half of the group would let ring out, "Tastes great" And in response the other half of the group would yell out, "less filling!" [from a Miller Beer advertisement]. We went back and forth like this for a while as everyone broke out in laughter.

In this instance, the group finds a common referent, the phrase from the Miller beer advertisement, on which to connect. The context is important, as it involves a large group of unfamiliar people engaged in a rather unstructured activity. The use of the catch phrase from the Miller advertisement in this case is like a volleyball being tossed from side to side. In the process, the participants have shared in a pleasant, perhaps humorous game. In finding this common ground they have declared their connectedness. The use of the content of the advertisement, in this case, serves as social integrator.

Contexts that create the need for a "home" language, such as eating in restaurants, talking to co-workers, or participating in various social activities, may lead participants to comment or evaluate the food, service or activity in the language of advertising. In the following examples, the individuals select the content of advertisements as a common ground on which to share an experience:

There were six of us eating dinner at a Creole cuisine restaurant. We ordered the Creole sauce rice along with our appetizers. When it arrived it looked and tasted like plain white rice. One woman remarked, "Where's the sauce?" A man in our party replied, "Where's the beef?"

When the new Coca Cola became available, everyone in my office was talking about it and they were [sic] anxious to try it. One veteran Coke drinker tasted the new Coke, so a coworker asked her, "How do you like it?" "I prefer the old Coke," she responded. A third person chimed in, "Teresa wants the real thing" [the real thing is a reference to another Coca Cola advertisement].

These uses, not emotionally laden or relationally dependent, enhance the interaction, allowing the individuals to enjoy their common experience in a collegial atmosphere.

ADVERTISING USE AS UNCOMMON GROUND

In other situations, individuals use advertising content to disassociate from particular cultural or social values. This takes the shape of a rather sophisticated play form. In the following example from a dinner party, the participants play "can you top this one."

At a dinner party attended by six adults, the conversation meandered on to the media. David, who is a physician, was making a point that one of the doctor dramas on television is medically inaccurate. As dessert was about to be served—a cake prepared by the host—David began to play off of this homemade dessert by joking about the preservatives and artificial ingredients of Sara Lee cakes. Beth, the hostess, stressing her contrary nature, played this game with David saying, "I'm one of those people who likes Sara Lee." Trying to one up her, David responded, "Well, nobody doesn't like Sara Lee."

The Sara Lee catch phrase is not inherently funny, nor is it meant to be in the context of the advertisement. David used the catch phrase to put distance between him and this typically middle American (and all the values that conjures up) product—the prepackaged frozen cake. Beth was being sarcastic when she claimed to like Sara Lee cake. She was, in essence, disassociating herself from the product and perhaps middle-class values (i.e., serving a previously frozen packaged cake with dinner). David had already set the stage for this disassociation when he questioned the lack of realism in the television medical drama. This provided him with further opportunity to clarify his disassociation from media values as he joined Beth in their verbal joust. The example indicates, paradoxically, that in order to disassociate from media values, one needs to have extensive knowledge about what is going on in the media.

ADVERTISING PLAY AND SOCIAL ROLES

In a pluralistic society, status or qualification can be conveyed not only through traditional roles, but also through the use of language or the short-lived common sense that is characteristic of advertising (Moscovici, 1981). In such a situation, a qualified member of society is one who uses advertising content in the context of performing a traditional social role. In the following examples, the play is other-directed and is hierarchical in nature. Advertising use may help to manage the social hierarchy that exists between and within groups. This is illustrated by the president of a corporation who is discussing with some of his company's managers a promotional umbrella imprinted with the corporate logo. At one point in the meeting the president offers this directive: "and don't leave home without them!" The corporate president asserts his authoritative role through the use of the American Express catch phrase. But in doing so, for a time, he becomes "one of the guys."

One informant reported a rather sarcastic use of advertising content when arguing with his lover:

> She questioned whether I loved her and I suggested that I was having the same problem. Then I said, in reference to this dilemma, "Is it real, or is it Memorex?"

In this case, he not only summed up the dilemma in one short sweet phrase, but in doing so he asserted his role in this power game. Glenn and Knapp (1987) referred to this as *playful aggression*, a situation in which one person does something to another. And in another example a student commented on a boring class and the substitute teacher who announces to the class, "It's No-Doz Time!"

Informants also use advertising in a self-directed manner in order to describe themselves, for example, to assert one's self in a social situation and to lay claim to a social identity:

> I was driving my son home from an appointment one evening when we drove past a gas station on the corner. My son asked if it was a full-service station to which I responded that I was a full-service dad.

He asked what I meant by that and I explained that I drive him everywhere and take care of him. Then, in order to drive the point home, I said, "I'm the dad that keeps you miling."

I was riding my bicycle with a friend one afternoon. We came to a stop sign and I rode across the street without stopping even though a car was oncoming. He had to stop and when he eventually caught up to me he mentioned that this was a pretty bold move on my part. I retorted, "there are bold pilots and old pilots, but no old, bold pilots." [This is a phrase from a GM advertisement featuring test pilot Chuck Yeager.]

EMOTIVE VALUE OF ADVERTISING USE

Altheide and Snow (1979) suggested that entertainment calls forth behaviors of emotion—love, hate, pride, tears, and laughter—and allows us to respond without embarrassment. Such play–acting transcends the page, speaker, or television screen. Similarly, the use of the content of advertising serves emotional needs of everyday life. Individuals, in their conversations, indicated feeling "nutty," "tired," "anxious," "sloppy," or "relieved," expressing these emotions through the language of advertising. In describing themselves, individuals exploit such advertising content for their personal needs. The following exemplifies the emotive quality of such advertising play:

I was sitting around the house with my son, looking for something to do. Sometimes when there's nothing to do we just get silly and start singing: "Sometimes I feel like a nut, sometimes I don't . . . Peter Paul Almond Joy has nuts, Mounds don't." Sometimes we mix the candies up on purpose, just to make it sound sillier.

As an expression of frustration over her car that was broken down on the side of a highway, one informant in exasperation remarked, "Oh what a feeling, Toyota." Another informant reported that while speaking to a friend about her anxiety over getting a new job she said, "I'm a mess . . . a real mess . . . A chocolate mess" (from an M&Ms advertisement).

MEDIA COMPLICITY IN ADVERTISING USE

Carey (1986) wrote about the familiarity of a story, referring to the journalist's understanding of the audience's familiarity with certain public figures. Although, he was not referring to familiarity with advertising catch phrases, the understanding to which Carey referred—that of the journalist and audience—of that familiarity is similar. Describing the audience's response to media symbols, Allen (1982) said, "familiar forms enter into the individual's reasoning process and allow them in the context of everyday conversation to draw quick parallels between situations without analysis by calling up a well known symbol to connote the parallel role of a less known personality in another situation" (108).

In a larger sense, as advertising is media content, its use as a reference in other media contexts, like newspaper articles, is a form of meta-media; media content turning inward. The concept of *meta-media* may have its greatest impact in the area of social learning. As media figures use the content of advertising, they sometimes are doing more than simply connecting to the culture through common referents. They may inadvertently be teaching their audiences something about the culture at large. In some cases the social learning has to do with the efficacy of products, and sometimes advertising is used as critical commentary about American culture, the capitalist system, mass media in general, or the advertising system. And although sometimes that commentary is highly critical, other times it is offered in good humor. For example, in a review of a new model Honda automobile, the newspaper reporter claims, "This Japanese automaker is trying to do to journalists what Maytag claims to do to washer repairmen." Later in the same review, under the heading of "Outstanding Praise," he states: "The gearshift's equally wonderful. It glides from first to second, to third, fourth, fifth and—zoom! The folks at Toyota like to shout, 'Oh what a feeling!' Ha, if they only knew."

Television programs like *Seinfeld, The Simpsons,* and *The Drew Carey Show,* to name a few, are peppered with references to products and advertising. In order to bring meaning to the news or entertainment programming, the writer must make certain assumptions about the audience. Understandably, not willing to risk losing readership or viewership, the writer may search for the phrase which some might consider the least objectionable. Carey (1975) referred to such an effort as a "profound collaboration" (147). However, it is only sometimes that the catch phrase or other advertising reference may appear in the media. Therefore, when a newspaper headline like "Where's the Beefski" appears in the "hard news" section, the reader knows this is a play on the Wendy's fast food restaurant advertisement and that the article is about international politics. In the case of a journalist or headline writer, she or he assumes the reader will understand the dual meaning implied in the use. In using familiar phrases, media writers make an assumption that the audience is aware of the advertising reference being used, so that as Carey said, the audience would grasp the dual meaning in the sentence. For example, an anchor on CNBC, the cable business channel, says in reference to their quarterly earnings, "Allstate stockholders may not feel like they're in good hands as the company announced lower earnings."

Allen (1982) spoke to this collaborative effort when he said, "The inherent effects of the mass communications process per se are neither consensus nor conflict producing but depend on the content and use of that content by audiences" (109). It is readily acknowledged that media popularize phrases that quickly pass into the language and for a time are used as similes and metaphors. The following example appears in a *Wall Street Journal* review of the ill-fated XFL football league: "What we saw Monday night, however, reminded us more than anything of the Energizer Bunny, the little pink rabbit with the drum who keeps going and going and going." Or in a very interesting twist, a *Business Week* magazine headline for an article on IBM's change in strategy regarding the consumer market for computers, "I'm not going to pay a lot for this Aptiva." Aptiva is IBM's brand name for computers marketed to consumers and the headline plays on another well-known catch phrase from an automobile muffler advertisement. A *New York Times* obituary for an executive of the American Express Company uses the headline, "Howard L. Clark Dead at 84; Did You Know Him? Maybe." This is a twist on the famous American Express advertising campaign in which spokespeople with familiar names with not-so-familiar faces asked, "Do you know me?"

MEDIA TRANSFORM ADVERTISEMENTS

Allen (1982) maintained that media content is transformed when it is used. News, basically factual content offered for its informational value, may actually be transformed for use as entertainment. Plummer (1971) would support this cultural role of advertising content as a handy expedient for communicating in other contexts. And because some of the content of advertising is taken as "absurd," as Plummer suggests, the media in some instances use advertising in a playful, ironic, or "absurd" manner (315).

The following series of uses depicts how a rather serious news story about a business scandal is offered as irony. The situation involves the E.F. Hutton Company, which was being investigated by the federal government for allegedly manipulating funds. In reference to this news story, Peter Jennings, ABC News anchor, said: "In other matters . . . the Justice Department talked as E.F. Hutton listened." And one National Public Radio reported says, "E.F. Hutton had to listen while the attorney general talked." After leading into the story with the familiar catch phrase from an E.F. Hutton advertisement, both accounts provide subsequent facts of the story in a straightforward manner. A story from the print media provides an example of similar use: "Some grim humor at the E.F. Hutton offices in the wake of the firm's guilty plea to charges that it defrauded its bankers: 'If they haven't heard of Hutton before, they've heard of us now,' anguished one broker." The same evening on which the E.F. Hutton story broke, a late night talk show host quipped, "How many of you listen to E.F. Hutton? [pause] How many of you wish you were deaf?"

The use can merely be a playful twist on a familiar phrase as in the course of a National Public Radio talk show several callers were offering their adulation to the guest, Mr. Rogers, the familiar host of a children's television program. After several callers spoke about their appreciation of Mr. Rogers' work, the interviewer, Diane Rehm, said, "You're just like Sara Lee . . . nobody doesn't like Mr. Rogers." In another play on the Sara Lee catch phrase, a *Wall Street Journal* interview with a mutual fund manager reports him saying with regard to Sara Lee stock, "Nobody loves Sara Lee."[2] Although it may be of little significance, this use adds vitality to the situation. In a similar, bordering on silly, reference to 8mm video technology a media critic lamented about purchasing the older form of video tape recorder when he wrote: "If you just bought an old-fashioned half-inch camcorder, you can slap yourself on the forehead and say, 'Gee, I could have had a V-8!'" In the following example a reviewer uses the classic Veg-O-Matic advertisement to describe a movie: "Why spend $5 to watch Jason, the hockey-masked psychopath of *Friday 13th—A New Beginning*, when for a few dollars more you can buy yourself a Veg-O-Matic? Jason chops and slices and cleaves, sure, but does he puree? Does he julienne?"

In some instances, the use of the advertising content is more than ironic, it is sarcastic and highly critical of a product, or the catch phrase may be transformed to criticize an individual. When the Coca-Cola Company changed its formula, the lead paragraph in a magazine article asked the question: "Coke is it, isn't it? The answer, hard as it may be to swallow is, well, not exactly." In another example, a media critic wrote the following in a newspaper column critical of the new product: "It's the unreal thing. The pause that depresses. It is not. It is something else again. Coca-Cola, which once said it would like to teach the world to sing in perfect har-mo-nee, is now hearing the chorus of discord about the fact that for reasons unfathomable to the normal human with a thirst to quench, Coke has changed its formula from the one America loves to the new one America isn't quite sure about."

The drama critic's use may be quite sarcastic, lacking the sensitivity shown during conversations in primary relationships, or more light-hearted uses displayed in other examples. In a review of a television remake of the play *Long Hot Summer*, the critic refers to Cybil

Shepherd as the "Maggie-the-Cat" figure and Don Johnson of *Miami Vice* as the "this-stud's-for-you" figure (a play on "this Bud's for you" slogan for Budweiser beer). And an article in the sports section questions why certain Olympic athletes are not among those doing advertisements, "smiling from a box of Wheaties, selling soft drinks that get America going or mouthwash to keep it kissable sweet?"

MEDIA USE OF ADVERTISING FOR SOCIAL LEARNING

When the media—news and entertainment—use the content of advertisements, they sometimes are doing more than connecting to the culture by simply joking around. They are teaching viewers, listeners, and readers something about the political, economic, or social system. In some cases, the social learning has to do with products, but sometimes on a more covert level advertising content is used as commentary about American culture and society. And although the use of advertising content as commentary may be highly critical, and perhaps cynical, other times it is offered in good humor. As examples, several newspaper articles about specific products use the content of an advertisement as commentary. In a magazine article about exercise equipment the writer uses the content of advertising to launch an attack on advertising. The article is critical of those products claiming to take weight off with little effort. The lead paragraph states:

> Quick and easy exercise routines remind me of the get something for practically nothing advertisements in trashy tabloids. The ads go something like: Get a complete physical workout WHILE YOU SLEEP!! With our new revolutionary system you can build muscles, lose weight and work off tension overnight WITHOUT LEAVING BED!!!

In this instance, the use serves as reinforcement that some products do not work as claimed or that advertising is deceptive. The context in which it is offered, however, is paradoxical. The reporter uses the content of an advertisement to castigate advertising. On a more covert level another lesson is being offered; that advertising lies, and reporters tell the truth. The later is reinforced when the reporter divulges the "truth" about the product that doesn't work as claimed. The use reinforces the importance of the reporter's role in U.S. society.

A sports writer follows the same idea; advertised products may not work as claimed. The approach is glib, but the intention is critical as the advertisement serves as a means by which to launch the diatribe.

> There's a commercial on cable TV advertising a fish sniff. A guy
> wearing sunglasses comes on in a boat, pushing a bottled product
> that attracts fish. I think it's called 'Eau de Croaker' and is just anoth-
> er product that makes the battle between man and fish that much
> fairer. For the price of $10.95 for walleye and $11.95 for large mouth
> bass, you can be assured of catching something every time out. The
> commercial ends by showing some grinning fool with his limit of 25
> dead fish. He owes his fishing success to one bottle of Chanel
> Number Five.

In this case, the reporter may be simply suggesting that there is no
easy way to catch fish and the use of such a product goes against the
grain of the American sportsman. The reporter may also be asserting
the importance of his role. This may be a particularly useful impres-
sion to make for the sports reporter who may not be taken as seriously
as his "hard news" brethren.

The content of an advertisement may help to ease the reader
into a political story as in the headline for a magazine article that read,
"How do the Russians Spell Relief?" When this example appeared,
there was a concurrent trend in advertising in which advertisements
parodied the Soviet system. In a newspaper article about this advertising fad, a business reporter uses the following epigram as a lead to her
story:

> In America, there's plenty of Lite Beer and you can
> always find a party.
> In Russia, Party always finds you.
>   —Russian [emigre] comedian Yakov Smirnoff
>   in commercial for Miller's Lite Beer.

The following provides an example of a newspaper columnist
presenting ironic social commentary about Americans' use of the
English language. Ironic use of advertising catch phrases are displayed
in the headline, the lead paragraph and the body of the story:

> Here it is, the conversation of the future:
> "Where's the beef?"
> "I can't believe I ate the whole thing."
>   "Bet you can't eat just one."
>   "You 'n' me, babe."
> It's been creeping up on us for years—designer conversation,
> franchised phraseology, quick frozen quips, fast phrase
> communication, McWords . . .

This confluence of familiar phrases continues in this attack on
advertising as a culprit in the deterioration of the English language.

It could get so popular that other ad campaigns will stick it in their slogans whether it makes sense or not.
Imagine it:
Nothing comes between me and me beef.
Ring around the beef.
Beef is it.
And the Panasonic Company will be slightly ahead of its beef.

Perhaps the nature of the media critic's job provides a plausible explanation why she or he would use as fodder for their columns the content of advertisements, or any other media content for that matter. In the following example, the critic seizes the opportunity to castigate not only technological determinism, but uses the article as a platform to criticize the advertising industry, alluding to some sinister use to which "Madison Avenue" might put stereo television. But it is emphasized that he, paradoxically, uses the content of advertising to criticize advertising. "After all, do we dream in mono? No, we dream in stereo [What is a hamburger . . . chopped ham? No, it's chopped steak (this phrase is a take on an A-1 Steak Sauce slogan), but that's another matter] . . ." In the eighth paragraph, advertising content is employed to reinforce the critic's position: "It's Double–Stuff Television—two, two, two sound tracks in one. Or actually two sound tracks in two, if the dang thing is working right." The reporter speaks to the inevitability of this application to the new technology in the resolution in the story. "The real effects of stereo won't be felt, however, until Madison Avenue has fully tooled up for this godsend. Those taunting teases the Double mint twins can come back and each get their own speaker. The snap, crackle and pop of Rice Krispies will sound like World War III. The Tidy Bowl man will adapt to the changing environment by—well, it's too horrible to contemplate. Besides, I might be able to get a whole other column out of this." In addition to making "good copy," each of these examples allows the reporter to distance himself from the subject on which he writes. In addition to the commentary the writer offers, there is a cultural critique that is simultaneously being offered. Similar to the sports reporter's use just described, the critic uses the advertisements to distance himself from the media on which he reports. The use of advertising suggests the media cannot manipulate the reporter, reinforcing his trustworthiness or credibility as a reporter.

CONCLUSION

The use of advertising—the circulation of its content in everyday life—is something that Americans take for granted. It is the ordinariness of this social practice that makes it significant. Garfinkel (cited in

Scannell, 1998) demonstrated in his "breaching experiments" that trust in the ordinary meaningfulness of talk in everyday contexts sustains trust in the meaningfulness of the everyday world as such. Verbal play with the content of advertising is a social practice that we take for granted based on the trust in the ordinary meaningfulness of talk. Along with other forms of media content, advertising functions to help maintain the social structure by promoting social conformity. Like many forms of play, informants' play showed varying degrees of creativity and inventiveness. In the case of their verbal play with the content of advertising, the meaning and importance of this activity goes beyond the desire to entertain.

Knowing the content of advertisements, and transforming that content for use in conversations is a function of advertising learned in childhood and refined in adulthood, and is one of the ways we consent to participate with its content. It is also a means of socially empowering the individual when advertising language enters everyday talk. Rather than "playing for no gain" there is a purpose to this use of advertising that is important to the moving equilibrium of social relationships. In some cases, this verbal play performs a mediating role, and in other cases individuals play to win. Advertising messages are so malleable that individuals twist and turn them—like improvisational jazz—to fit their needs. Clearly, with so many advertising messages available to individuals, a limited number find their way into everyday use. However, once a part of the common language, the content of advertising may not be as ephemeral as once thought.

Members of the media—reporters and entertainers—understand the importance of advertising as an efficient and effective way to appeal to individuals who come to the media for their news, information and entertainment. Reporters and editors, for example, understand that newspaper audiences may be comprised partially of "scanners" who may need to be lured into reading a story. Television newscasters recognize the need to cut through the "clutter" and partial misunderstanding of news and events by placing them in a context in which the meaning will be clear, yet concise. And, entertainers understand the need to relate to their audiences through familiar phrases and the need to be expedient in their communication.

The media use the content of advertising in an ironic and playful manner, but they use it in a sarcastic and mean spirited manner as well. Within this variety of uses there may be a range of meaning: little meaning when the familiar phrase is offered merely to catch attention as in a simple joke or in passing, to greater meaning when the reporter or media figure is trying to make a point critical to the message they are trying to convey. The media, just like individuals, use the content of advertising as social and political commentary that serves as a device for social learning.

Advertising content is a single element of our mass–mediated community. Individuals participate in a give and take with the media, and conversely the media participate in a give and take with audiences, such that the content becomes much like mass produced products. We select some of these products, for example, the content of advertising, and adopt some of the content for use in everyday life. It is not so much that we trust advertising; we do not. However, we do trust that it is going to be there and that it is one of the ingredients that sustains the meaningfulness of the everyday world.

ENDNOTES

1. See the Appendix for an explanation of the ethnographic methods utilized to describe and interpret the social uses of advertising presented in this chapter.
2. Based on the widespread recognition of the brand Sara Lee, the parent corporation, Consolidated Foods, decided to change its corporate name to Sara Lee.

PART III

7

THE CULTURAL SIGNIFICANCE OF ADVERTISING

Advertising plays a role within the financial economy that is rooted in the belief that it can move the excess of production through the system. In the process, advertising not only attempts to sell us goods and services, but also operates on the cultural level to provide symbolic associations between those goods and services, associated images, like those of media figures, and values related to the consumer's lifestyle. However, neither advertisers nor its social and cultural critics, from the political right or left, have clearly articulated advertising's role within the complexity of contemporary American culture. National consumer goods advertising does not carry with it the same hard sell as does other forms of advertising and sales promotion. Rather, national consumer goods advertising, like that for Coke or Pepsi, is part of the "soft sell" and hence may have greater cultural significance as we consume its images. National consumer goods advertising is "relatively placeless and timeless" and "highly abstracted and self-contained" (Schudson, 1984: 211).

An advertisement is a highly crafted piece of work that relies on a grab bag of creative techniques to engage the consumer in its discourse. And, advertising is unique among media content as it has a charge beyond the entertainment value and beautiful images—its intention is to sell or at least perform one of the hierarchical functions, like creating awareness or preference. In order to accomplish its goals, advertising operates within a magical system that is rooted in the early modern period when market fairs and religious Carnivals led to a social experience that elevated the consumer beyond the routine of their ordinary lives. Advertising is rooted in commerce, and the qualities of magic and fantasy continue to this day as part of its foundation. In contemporary society, distance from the source of production roots consumers in the sterile world of boxes and packaging, and breeds reliance on advertising's magic, not only as a source of information, but as a replacement for the tactility historically associated with the production of goods.

The marvel and wonder that advertising is imbued with veils a system of commerce that is less certain than it appears. Advertising's economic role is to stabilize the marketing system in America in order to keep the excess flow of goods moving from production to consumption. Based on overproduction and planned obsolescence, the consumer lifestyle in America, "keeping up with the Jones," has become the model for organizational life in America. But uncertainty is built into the system: Markets are unstable, technology changes rapidly, and consumers are fickle. With regard to the consumer, what this means is that advertising cannot manage their attitudes in ways marketers would like.

Even though consumers may consent to participate in the wonder and magic of advertising, the advertising may not produce the desired outcome. Meaning is an allusive quality as consumers employ tactics of both complicity and resistance as they engage with advertising and as they carry it into social discourse. Advertising meanings are polysemic allowing for variable interpretations of its texts. And within those "readings" of advertising's texts, it is important to acknowledge the possibility that as part of the natural order, an advertisement may be rendered meaningless. Consumers do not necessarily read "against" a text, that is to say, they are not always oppositional in their approach to advertising. There are, however, a variety and range of possibilities with regard to consumer interpretation of advertising texts. Within that variety and range consumers may find an advertisement meaningful or they may find it meaningless. Ambiguity and vagueness also have to be considered within the continuum of meaning in which consumers operate.

What work does advertising do in the culture and what work do we do with it were questions raised at the beginning of this book. Using ethnographic methods I described how in the course of our everyday lives we temporally move among multiple realities. Media consumption—another reality itself—provides opportunities to enter into, yet, other realities.[1] In order to negotiate our way through the labyrinth of media consumption, individuals employ tactics—ingenious ways—to deal with the political dimensions of their everyday lives. These tactics become social practices or routines through which we interpret advertising for our own use. Sometimes we reintegrate aspects of advertisements into our everyday lives. Other times advertising, so to speak, goes in one ear and out the other.

THINKING ABOUT ADVERTISING

When an advertisement appears on the screen interrupting a program or appears on the page—before, in the middle of, or after editorial matter—sometimes we pay attention to it; sometimes we do not. Advertising provides an opportunity to turn away from what is before us, a form of practiced inattention. Turning our attention inward takes place during media consumption and under many other routine experiences multiple times during the day. Similar to driving a car to work in a routine manner, when consuming media we sometimes drift off, but we do not, metaphorically, take our hands off the wheel. Familiarity with advertisements, or parts thereof, serve as a cue, signaling that it is safe to turn away from what is before us. Advertisers may not appreciate these "mental commercials," but moving back and forth between multiple realities is nevertheless a part of the process of consuming media and the routine practices of everyday life. Such experiences are not media-centric, that is, they do not only take place during media consumption. Therefore, this routine practice—turning inward and away from what is before us—is something to which we have been enculturated, and we have carried this practice into media consumption and away from media consumption.

Moreover, it is the creative devices themselves that advertisers routinely change in order to stimulate interest in the advertisement that provide those signals to mentally zap the advertisements. For example, one creative tactic is to produce advertisements that do not look like advertisements, what Sivulka (1998) called noncommercials. "Experts predict that as commercials become larger and more entertaining, it will become more difficult to tell the difference between an ad and a program" (407). There is a certain sense of irony watching advertising operate at the cultural level, as the invocation of the social practices of avoidance and resistance is taken for granted as being trivial. But far from trivial the practice of turning away is a significant part of the cultural experience in which we engage when we consume commercial media.

What happens when we engage in reverie while attending to commercial media? We sometimes conjure up memories and anticipate the future. And when viewers, listeners, and readers mentally leave for a few moments the "unreality" of mass media, they enter another imaginary world, yet one that is highly social. The imaginary world includes scenes, situations, characters, roles, and the social relationships and hierarchy that exist in the actual world. Perhaps most interestingly we do not always fantasize about driving expensive cars or living in luxurious houses, although sometimes we do. More often we think about practical matters. So, the advertising that feeds back to us an idealized vision of American life serves as a cue to drive the individual into an imaginary social world that is to a great extent driven by the personal and the practical. People think about their jobs, relationships, and general well-being in the context of pseudosocial interactions that replicate everyday life. They also think critically about advertising as is evident in their self-talk.

The inward experience of advertising is highly subjective, a cultural world bound by memories and anticipations. The cultural practice of turning away, a form of resistance or avoidance and complicity is a culturally learned tactic that represents the struggle between advertiser and consumer. Advertisers do not like it when consumers are mentally away, or physically removed for that matter, and they go to extremes in order to gain and maintain attention. After all, how can advertising fuel the economic system when consumers have their eyes on the screen or page, but their minds elsewhere? One of the primary concerns of advertisers, for example, is zapping of commercials with the use of a remote control or zipping past the commercials that have been recorded for playback on a VCR. Through practiced avoidance, consumers sometimes covertly zap the advertisements anyway. Ideologically, consumers do more than merely avoid advertising as they sometimes resist its messages. This resistance takes the form of self-talk as the consumer counteracts what is being placed before them.

In their inner world an advertisement works at the ideological level as individuals perhaps avoid its message entirely by thinking about something unrelated, perhaps a memory. Or, they may be complicit as there may be some tangential connection between the stream of consciousness or fantasy and the advertisement. Ideology is also at work as individuals engage in self-talk where they evaluate products, advertisements or some related aspect of the economic system. Advertising works to keep its message or perhaps some specific aspect of the advertisement present in the mind of the consumer. This practice keeps our world before us and contributes to the postmodern experience of ordinary existence. Although there might not be comfort in the experience, there are stabilizing and destabilizing forces at work. As the struggle between the advertiser and consumer ensues, the predictability of advertising becomes variable as consumers employ a variety and range of tactics as they reintegrate it (or not) into their inner worlds.

During media consumption, when the individual for a time is in a dreamlike state, their memories and anticipations present opportunities to rework the content of advertising. The reworking of content is a form of negotiation in which the individual is not necessarily a passive or dominant participant, but rather engages in a system of moving equilibrium. This ongoing correspondence contributes to the social order and perhaps disrupts this order by serving as a self-socialization mechanism. As the correspondence is ongoing, it roots the struggle between advertiser and consumer within a multi-dimensional matrix of meanings and discourses giving this social practice its own history. The significance lies not merely in the way we engage with an advertisement, but how we operate within the ideological matrix of myriad advertisements that are presented to us everyday. Therefore, it is not just about the way we engage with an advertisement, but how we operate within the ideological matrix of myriad advertisements and the meanings they attempt to convey and the meanings we construct on a regular basis. It is our routine correspondence, a routine cultural practice, within the ideological matrix that supports both the cultural stability and instability that arises.

The inward activity associated with stream of consciousness and fantasy behavior is not merely about what is real and what is not real—two modes of subjective experience. The ideological framework for this interaction is an important part of understanding the politics of streaming. Stream of consciousness and fantasy behavior are opportunities to resist or comply with the dominant ideology that is offered in an advertisement. Streaming presents opportunities to oppose the dominant forces in the culture and it may be a means to attempt to exert cultural resistance. I say attempt because resistance may not always be successful and the individual may choose to "read" the advertisement, as S. Hall (1980) suggested, "with" the dominant ideology. We can see oppositionality at work when individuals in their stream question certain aspects of an advertisement and the system in which it exists. The subjective modality of stream of consciousness activity that may appear quite mobile, perhaps volatile, represents an opportunity to at least partially affect consumers' own reality.

Stream of consciousness activity treats ideology at the level of social formation, a social practice that produces experience with the strings of connotation and their representation given by advertisers. Although the thoughts contained in the stream of consciousness may appear to be private, this activity is a public one in the sense that the contents of the thoughts and fantasies are culturally constituted. In other words, what we think about is in the public domain. In this sense, as hegemony theory would suggest, advertisers get to frame the discussion or set the agenda, but they may not get to control the outcome. Advertising is a part of the system that guides us toward making sense of our world. As such it serves as a container for streaming and fantasizing about things on our minds and it presents opportunities to adjust our subjective reality as a function of self-talk. This process, however, keeps culture before us. And, we can see within the social practice of streaming and fantasizing while consuming advertising that keeping the culture ever present in our minds must be a stressful aspect of our postmodern existence.

Fiske (1989) pointed up the need to recognize the "socialization of the interior" as an important part of the micropolitical world. He said:

> The most micro of micropolitics is the interior world of fantasy. The preservation of fantasy as an interior place beyond the reach of ideological colonization, and the ability to imagine oneself acting differently in different circumstances, may not in itself result in social action, whether at the micro or macro level, but it does constitute the ground upon which any such action must occur. It is difficult to conceive of a movement for social change that does not depend on people's ability to think of themselves and their social relations in ways that differ from those preferred by the dominant ideology. (190)

DREAMING ABOUT ADVERTISING

There is a synergy within the imaginary social world of the individual between stream of consciousness processes and dreams. Media figures from advertising that individuals speak about in their imaginary social relationships that appear in advertising are also among the media figures that show up in the individual's dreams. There are connections between imagining and dreaming about and through advertising content. The interaction within the imaginary world of the individual has been described as a pseudosocial interaction as media figures and products that appear in advertisements become intertwined, however, these connections should not reinvigorate the effects debate. It is reductionist to claim that advertising showing up in conversations, thoughts, and fantasies as well as our dreams is an effect. From a cultural perspective, what is important is how we reintegrate the content of advertising into our conversations, thoughts, fantasies, and dreams. In other words, an important, but neglected area is what we do with advertising after it appears on the screen or page and how it enters the social discourse of everyday life.

Rather than having direct effects on people's behavior, advertising is a highly negotiated form of mass communication. As its content becomes integrated into the dream world or reintegrated into the waking world through dream sharing, advertising and elements within its content are greatly compromised. For example, in the dream world, media figures are recognizable, but their social interactions, social relationships, and social roles are altered. The research presented in this book points out that media figures are the only characters in dreams to consistently have their social status altered. There are psychoanalytic explanations, like Freud's concept of condensation that may account for replacing one character with another, which may serve as a partial explanation for this phenomenon. From a cultural perspective, however, the transposition of the media figure within the dream world offers a level of familiarity and intimacy that is much more equal than is possible in waking life.

When individuals talk about their dreams, which in American culture they sometimes do, they (the dreams) serve as a resource that has cultural significance. There is a social aspect to recounting a dream about a celebrity to another individual. And, we negotiate the culture by filtering the kinds of dreams we will tell to others. By the same token, choosing not to tell dreams that suggest the individual dreamer is overly materialistic may also be one way of negotiating the culture. The research points out that individuals are overwhelmingly convinced that they must dream about advertising, but the dreams they recount do not support their belief, at least not to any great extent. Their selectivity in the recounting of dreams has an important cultural dimension. Products, media figures, and other elements within advertisements are utilized sparingly and strategically when recounting dreams.

Such cultural referents, like catch phrases from advertisements, make for expedient communication. They are a way to make what we say meaningful to others and to cut to the chase. The choices that individuals are making are just one of the ways in which they speak through the cultural referents that have been given them. How consumers speak through those cultural referents may be an expression of their cultural resistance toward the dominant forces of advertising. In this sense, the dream world and the recounting of dreams in the waking world are much like the way we operate in various actual social contexts: picking and choosing what we are going to say and how we are going to say it and measuring it against what we think others will think of us. The social value of the advertisements, products, and media figures may be summed up in the ways in which we incorporate them, or choose not to, within our dream world and waking social world during dream sharing. There may be a connection between the repetitive nature of advertising and its relative absence within the dream world. It may be that repetition reduces psychological tension. As we become familiar with an advertisement and elements of its contents there is little need to dream about it.

IMAGINARY RELATIONSHIPS WITH MEDIA FIGURES

A related experience of advertising in everyday life is the subjective nature of imaginary social relationships. Sherry (1987) said "by linking reference figure to product, it may provide us with both rationale and tactics for negotiating the uncertain contexts of consumer choice" (445). As chapter 5 points out, individuals do much more with media figures than use them as "guides" regarding purchase decisions. Advertisers may present media figures as a model of expertise or for emulation that consumers are supposed to utilize as a guide in order to encourage their decision making. However, the presentation of the media figure within an advertisement is only a point of struggle—resistance and complicity—whereby consumers use the media figures that are given, but to their own ends. In this sense advertising is taken as incomplete and therefore it does not present meaning whole.

Involvement in an imaginary social relationship with a media figure appearing in an advertisement is some times deep and abiding. Individuals carry into their imaginary social relationships many of the qualities of actual social relationships. Such imaginary relationships may last a very long time and the media figure's appearance in an advertisement may be used to adjust the relationship, enhancing or detracting from it. In other words, these are socially patterned experiences. A recurring theme in this book is the predictability of media figures—for better or worse you can count on them being there. The presence of media figures in advertising lends itself to cultural stability in the sense that their presence is something we can count on. However, familiarity may breed contempt as individuals use appearances to question what is before them. In this sense, the appearance of media figures in advertising lends itself to reality maintenance.

As these imaginary social relationships sometimes are long term, deep, and abiding, and because in many cases they begin in some other media context other than advertising, imaginary relationships are quite complex. This is especially so when you consider that television, magazines, radio, and other forms are the mediating forces. These mediating forces provide multiple opportunities to fill in the gaps or expand on what might otherwise be seen as one-dimensional characters. A media figure's appearance in an advertisement may be like catching up with an old friend. And in this sense imaginary social relationships parallel actual social relationships. We have feelings—both good and bad—about media figures. And appearances in advertising can provide fuel for those feelings. The appearance in an advertisement also might be used to gauge the media figure's career or status and as such it might be used to alter the media figure's status in the mind of the consumer.

From an advertiser's perspective, the use of media figures in advertising can be fairly shaky ground as the potential for a media figure's public fall from grace has affected the brand image of more than one product. Consumers use appearances in advertising as an opportunity to make judgments about a media figure's career or popularity. Like other aspects of the imaginary social world, media figures present opportunities to process the ideological forces within society, for example, to raise questions about the celebrity system. Consumers use appearances of media figures in advertising as a point of negotiation between what we are suppose to think about a media figure and how in our imaginary social worlds we do think about them.

THE CIRCULATION OF ADVERTISING IN EVERYDAY CONVERSATIONS

Familiarity that comes through repetition of advertising serves the imaginary social world by encouraging multiple meanings that consumers derive from its content. The self-talk that is associated with the appropriation of meaning helps to ground individuals in the social world. In the actual social world, as its content circulates through everyday life, advertising familiarity becomes a point of commonality. In using the language of advertising we conform to a social agreement with regard to the ways in which we communicate through the "home" language. The use of catch phrases, slogans, and the like, is a predictable part of the ways in which we communicate and the ways in which we attempt to create a shared culture—advertising is something we have in common. Advertising is a disposable commodity—we consume some of it, use it up and throw it away. The continual flow of advertising as it clutters the commercial media helps to sustain the "home" language. And like much else in our "disposable" society, advertising referents are heaped on the metaphoric landfill. This is a point of much cultural criticism directed toward advertising. However, it is important to keep in mind that consumers do not use the language of advertising as advertisers give it to them. And, to that degree, advertising is a potential source of social empowerment. Culturally, this social practice—using advertising in the context of social discourse—is something we learn in childhood and refine in adulthood. And, at the very least, the use of advertising content in the course of everyday life does liven up conversations. There is something of social value in this use of advertising for the individual, and there appears to be little to support the connection between the use of advertising in everyday life and its effects on purchasing behavior.

Similar to the ways in which the content of advertising is reworked in the inner world, in social discourse individuals invariably twist and turn advertising's catch phrases and use them out of the context in which they were originally intended. This form of "textual poaching" is one of the ways we use what is given to us by the commercial media, but we twist it and turn it as we use it to our own ends. In this way we may resist or avoid what is directly handed to us, however, there is a compromise at work. We do incorporate the language of advertising into our everyday lives, and to this extent we take what is given, although we do not take it literally.

The commercial media support this system as they incorporate aspects of advertising into other forms—news and entertainment programming. The media use advertising for similar reasons; it is an expedient means of communicating. A form of cultural shorthand, the content of advertising serves as a quick, sometimes clever means of expression and as listeners or readers we usually get the point. Indeed, some people are so adept at incorporating catch phrases and the like into their conversations that there is a certain status that is associated with this clever use of language. And, because we understand the catch phrases and slogans have been transformed from their intended use, we can see people in the media—newscasters and reporters, among others—use the content of advertising in order to connect with audiences, offer social commentary, or for social learning.

Advertisements start with us, that is to say that creative people in the industry mine the culture for values that we already hold close. However, the way those values are presented is a refracted image of society that may represent an ideal way of life. What happens when people consume those advertisements is another story. The process of communication becomes quite unpredictable. It is true that sometimes consumers take advertising to heart and find meaning that may translate into the sale of a product or service. But it is just as likely that the advertisement will go "in one ear and out the other." There is a middle ground, too, in which elements of the advertisement get through. Those elements, for various reasons, are reintegrated into our stream of consciousness, fantasies, dreams, and imaginary social relationships. These elements may also circulate through the culture as the language of advertising permeates everyday conversations. But the variety and range of these uses is great and provides a view of advertising's work in the culture and the work we do with it as one that is both resistant to and complicit with the dominant ideology that advertisers convey.

ENDNOTES

1. Imaginary social worlds parallel the actual world of everyday life. In this sense we live in multiple realities.

8

A ROUTE THROUGH THE PARADOXES OF ADVERTISING IN EVERYDAY LIFE

Advertising, Schudson (1984) said, is a "reflection of a common symbolic culture. Advertising, whether or not it sells cars or chocolate, surrounds us and enters into us, so that when we speak we speak in or with reference to the language of advertising and when we see we may see through schemata that advertising has made salient for us" (210). Advertising as a social practice of everyday life extends the cultural significance that Schudson described. Beyond the common system of cultural symbols, advertising does its work through the social interactions that exist within actual social relationships and in the psuedosocial interactions within our imaginary social world. As it is interconnected with the mass communication system and consumption capitalism, advertising is only one purveyor of cultural symbols, and it is only one contributor to the social and pseudosocial interactions of the individual. Advertising, because of its unique qualities that are unlike other forms such as news and entertainment, provides an ideal environment in which to view the interactions associated with media consumption practiced on a routine basis.

Unlike news or entertainment programming, advertising is overtly propagandistic. Simply put: Its purpose is to sell. It may inform and entertain along the way, but at the end of the day, its intentions are to impress the consumer with a brand image or meaningful association, or to communicate some attribute of the product and to claim that attribute is perhaps better than those available through alternative or competitive products or services. Advertising is interested in having an effect (sales), otherwise it fails to fulfill the obligation of its economic role to keep the excess of production moving through the system. Advertising's economic role, therefore, is an attempt to stabilize, if not control, the marketplace.

The effects tradition in which advertising theory is rooted conceives of the audience as the passive recipient of its messages.

> Theorists have suggested, for example, that critical capacities are worn down by the "the pervasive and irresistible flow of media messages," that mass media are increasingly "subtle and effective," that media communication is essentially of an "addictive and habitual character," that new media drawing on senses rather than thought are themselves the message. (Gamson, 1994: 200)

This theoretical perspective places much power on the "text" of advertising, and it is based on the assumption that what the text says is what the audience receives and ultimately acts on. Theoretically, the effects hierarchy—awareness, knowledge, liking, preference, and purchase—conceptualizes advertising's effects in a linear manner. Advertisers base their hopes on this model that projects effects at the end of the line.

THE TRANSMISSION MODEL

The linearity of advertising's effects is based on the "transmission" model of communication in which a powerful sender (advertiser) transmits a message to a receiver, the end product of which is some intended action on the part of the consumer. The advertising industry places much faith in this model even though markets are not as stable as producers would like them to be. Volatility is built into the system, and the idea that advertising provides the necessary control mechanism is a myth. The variety and range of consumer reactions to and experiences of advertising described in this volume speak to the variability of advertising's potential or lack thereof to communicate effectively. As has been stressed here, things may not be quite as stable as advertisers would like. Advertisers cling to this transmission model regarding advertising's effectiveness, and they take comfort in the fact that it offers a complete story. By that I mean to suggest that advertisers believe their own fairy tale. In this postmodern world of uncertainties, this chapter serves as a partial theory of the way advertising works in the culture and the work we do with it.

THE RITUAL MODEL

Carey (1989) presented an alternative to the "effects" model of communication that has some application to advertising. He referred to this model as the "ritual" model of communication. It is through the rituals of communication, he claimed, that a shared culture is created. For example, I described how talking to others through the language of advertising is a routine behavior that results in experiences that are shared, and hence, the creation of a common culture. There is great potential to create a shared culture as the floodgates of advertising provide a steady flow of materials from which to choose, and myriad ways—infinite variability—in which consumers may reintegrate advertising (or not) into their everyday lives. Ang (1996) was critical of Carey's ritual model, which she claimed views communication as the center around which everything else revolves. As Ang put it, Carey sees communication as culture (the title of his book). "Without communication, there can be no culture, and hence, no meaningful social reality" (166). Ang maintained there are problems with Carey's theoretical argument and offers modifications that are consistent with the summary of empirical research presented in the previous chapter.

Carey emphasized ritual order and common culture in a way that assumes this "can and should" be achieved. Communication in Carey's model functions as the glue that binds us through the construction of continuity and commonality of meanings. In other words communication is at the center of things. Because of its very nature, in particular its repetitiveness, advertisements it would seem provide ample opportunities to fuel the construction of continuity and commonality of meanings. Semiotic models of communication, like Carey's ritual model, privilege the construction of meaning where "communication is conceived as a social practice of meaning production, circulation and exchange" (Ang, 1996: 166). This is reflected in Carey's ritual view of the sharing and shaping of a common culture through communication. Communication, in Carey's view, is the centralizing function in that there can be no culture without communication. "Ritual order" and "commonality" are key ingredients in the development of shared culture—the social cement that binds us.

Fiske (1989) amplified this when he substituted the word *consumer* with the term "circulator of meanings" (27). For Fiske, "meanings are the only elements in the process that can be neither commodified nor consumed: meanings can be produced, reproduced, and circulated only in that constant process we call culture" (27). Therefore, in order to see advertising at work in the culture, it is imperative to focus on the site of the struggle through which a shared culture is created. This is accomplished by viewing routine practices that comprise a dynamic process in which individuals engage with advertising in the course of their ordinary existence.

POSTMODERN CONSUMPTION CAPITALISM

Fiske's approach to the meaning-making system is similar to the uses-and-gratifications theorists who assigned, perhaps, too much power to the individual rendering a text, like an advertisement, powerless to impose meanings. I present a compromise position that operates between the view that the consumer (or circulator of meaning) is so powerful as to render an advertisement meaningless and the industry view of a passive consumer who is at the mercy of the all-powerful advertisement. We may not be able to determine when or if equilibrium is ever reached, but through the empirical evidence presented in this book we can see the work advertising does in the culture and the work we do with it. It is the dynamic between the two that creates a moving equilibrium that is represented in the uses of advertising in the every-day life of the individual.

Within this dynamic interaction between advertising and the individual, cultural forces suggest there is social utility in the "texts" of advertisements as they are sometimes used in the context of everyday life. In this sense the individual is socially empowered through the use of advertising's content. That empowerment is one part of the dynamic interaction that takes place within an advertising system about which consumers have little control. Advertisers dominate the system that makes commercial messages pervasive in U.S. society. The advertising system operates within a matrix that is controlled by advertisers, but within which individuals have great latitude in which to work with or against the messages conveyed through myriad media. In this sense, it is important to stress that the "text" of an advertisement or parts thereof may be absorbed and may be embedded in our imaginary world for a long time. On the other hand, individuals through their social interactions with others display other forms of empowerment that operate within the dimensions of the advertising matrix. Based on the social forces of everyday life, consumers reintegrate some of those advertising messages into social contexts altering the messages from their intended meaning. The "text" does get inside thoughts, fantasies, and dreams, and may be offered up in social discourse, and in this sense advertising operates within the multiple realities of everyday life. This compromise position extends S. Hall's (1980) notion of reading with, against, or negotiating meaning within a text and views advertis-ing's hegemony within the complexity of social relationships that extend beyond media consumption.

THE CONTINUUM OF MEANING

Ang (1996) maintained that the shared meanings to which Carey referred may be based on a false construct. Within the construct, Carey privileged meaning and meaningfulness over meaninglessness.

> Or to put it in the terminology of communication theory: a radically semiotic perspective ultimately subverts the concern with (successful) communication by foregrounding the idea of "no necessary correspondence" between the Sender's and the Receiver's meanings. That is to say, not success, but failure to communicate should be considered "normal" in a cultural universe where commonality of meaning cannot be taken for granted. (Ang, 1996: 167)

In expressing her concern for the notion of shared meanings, Ang acknowledged the importance of accommodating texts that are rendered meaningless. This position is supported by the descriptions of individuals who are confused or for various reasons reject the advertisements they see, hear, or read, thus rendering them meaningless. S. Hall said:

> If meaning is not an inherent property of the message, then the Sender is no longer the sole creator of meaning. If the Sender's intended message doesn't "get across," this is not a "failure in communications" resulting from unfortunate "noise" or the Receiver's misinterpretation or misunderstanding, but because the Receiver's active participation in the construction of meaning doesn't take place in the same ritual order as the Sender's. And even when there is some correspondence in meanings constructed on both sides, such correspondence is not natural but is itself constructed, the product of a particular articulation, through the imposition of limits and constraints to the openness of semiosis in the form of "preferred readings," between the moments of "encoding" and "decoding". (167)

For Ang, the failure to communicate is taken as a "normal" part of the process where Carey's commonality of meaning cannot be taken for granted.

I have found with regard to the ways individuals experience advertising in the course of their everyday lives that meaning operates on a continuum. A continuum of meaning begins with the idea that there may be no meaning in an advertisement; it is simply not relevant, entertaining, or does not strike the senses. In this sense, euphemistically speaking, much advertising goes in one ear and out the other. On the other hand, the power of an advertisement's aesthetic value cannot be denied, as sometimes, under some uncontrollable circumstances, people find relevance in an advertisement. This relevance might have to do with the simple desire for a product, and it might have to do with the aesthetics of the advertisement. Relevance may emerge through the copy, a catch phrase or jingle, and it might have to do with a media figure depicted in the advertisement to whom the individual is attracted or whom the individual knows from some other media context. With regard to the production of meaning, Gamson (1994) wrote of the importance of triangulating the focus on the audience, producer, and text:

> Negotiating the tug-of-war led me to privilege neither audience, producer, nor text, but to focus instead on the moments and mechanisms of linkage between producers, audiences, and texts. The negotiation suggested fruitful places for investigation: the activity of collective interpretation and the limitations set on meanings by the text; how audiences are taken into account in production activity; the gaps between the codes of senders and receivers of cultural meaning. The analysis zeroes in on meaning creation, both as "problematic" and as "work." (202)

The production of meaning may be seen as problematic when an advertiser intentionally creates what might be referred to as an obscure advertisement (from an advertiser's point of view meaningless advertisements can create emotional reactions so they can still be quite effective). The noncommercial, a technique referred to in the previous chapter, would be one such example. In a noncommercial, the advertiser uses music, color, and vague images to create a sensory connection between the advertisement and the consumer. In this sense the receiver would not cognitively process the advertisement, but would emotionally experience the advertisement. With regard to meaning creation this is what Gamson referred to as *work*. The objective of such a noncommercial is not to render its text meaningful, but rather to provide an experience.

It is also possible that an advertiser creates a rational advertisement that is to be understood as meaningful, regardless of whether the consumer "reads" with or against it. Consumers' reading of an advertisement as meaningful or meaningless is based on the social practices in which they engage. Consumers can read meaning into an advertisement based on its contextual relevance to their lives. They can also dismiss the advertisement. And ambiguity and vagueness play a key role in the meaning-making process. For a variety of reasons, meaning-making may have to do with viewing or reading practices, as through learned inattention, for example, the receiver may not get the meaning inherent in the advertisement, thus rendering the advertisement meaningless. Ironically, in this instance, it is quite possible that a meaningless advertisement may be experienced as emotionally satisfying. Conversely, a perfectly coherent message may be misunderstood or rendered meaningless by a viewer or reader who is involved in her or his own stream of consciousness during media consumption. And, misunderstanding or meaninglessness can result when the process of media consumption is interrupted; for example, when an individual turns to talk to someone else in the room interrupting their focus on the advertisement. Ambiguity and vagueness, subjects that I initially addressed in chapter 2, are forms of strategic waffling in which advertisers offer up, not just multiple meanings through puns, but "indeterminate use of meaning, in which no definite meanings can be pinned down, creating a vague and indefinable aura" (Meyers, 1994: 67).

And it is also possible that an advertiser gets across to the consumer the message intended, thus rendering it a meaningful reading of the "text." The continuum of meaning is not a set of fixed points, but suggests that there is an indeterminate variety and range of reactions and experiences we have with and through advertising. These variations go largely unseen as they take place within our daydreams, fantasies, night dreams, our imaginary social worlds and through the language we take for granted when we speak to one another. The continuum of meaning is dynamic, quite fluid, as we actively move within the parameters of meaningfulness and meaninglessness. Newer forms of advertising stimulate activity along the continuum, keeping it ever active.

NEW FORMS OF ADVERTISING

As new forms of creative and technical possibilities emerge, advertising adapts its ever-changing relationship to consumers. The following is a list of some recent innovations:

- Longer commercials (85 seconds) that are highly entertaining
- Same-day advertising, produced and aired the same day to add an air of freshness
- Advertisements that do not look like ads (e.g., Energizer batteries)
- Product placements in television and films
- Cross-promotions and tie-ins
- Infomercials or program-length commercials
- Commercials placed at the beginning of video rentals
- Direct mail video or video catalogues
- Interactive Internet advertising (Sivulka, 1998: 407-411)

These newer forms represent a continuation of the cat and mouse game, a dynamic between advertiser and consumer, which is a function of the ever-changing advertising landscape. For example, the reality show *The Runner* in which a contestant attempts to cross the country undetected, is structured in such a way that it embeds a subtle form of advertising within the show's content.[1] In the course of the proposed program, developed by Matt Damon and Ben Affleck, the contestant is directed to purchase a Big Mac and fries at McDonalds. Or he or she might be instructed to purchase a latte at Starbucks or place a call on his or her Nokia cell phone or make an ATM withdrawal at a Citibank-Chase machine. This technique integrates the product into the story line creating a form of organic product placement. Although product placements are not a new concept, advertisers recognize that consumers are apt to use their remote controls to avoid commercials as they surf the myriad channels that exist today (Carter, 2001). Stealth-like advertisements are just one more attempt to reach an audience that may avoid or resist advertisings' messages.

In another twist on postmodern advertising, the idea of virtual product placements has come of age. Advertisers can now drop products into programs after they have been produced. This technique is in use in TV sports, like baseball and football, whereby a sponsor's name and logo may magically appear behind home plate or across the first down stripe. The object of virtual placement is to combat "zap happy" TV viewers, because they cannot fast-forward past the advertisements, as the advertisements are now part of the program. Additionally, when programs go into syndication, a can of Coke, for example, can easily be replaced with a Pepsi can (Lefton, 2001). In a variation on the virtual product placement theme, a new genre of computer game is being developed as an advertising vehicle. These computer games embed logos and product names or featured products, like the game Dodge Speedway that features Dodge automobiles. Other major advertisers are joining the interactive gaming movement including: Ford, Radio Shack, General Motors, Toyota, Proctor & Gamble, and Sony Entertainment (Marriot, 2001).

The interconnectedness between advertising and other aspects of everyday life can be seen in an Italian trend toward advertising in hospitals. A law passed in 1999 allows for advertising in corridors and waiting rooms. Advertisers have expressed concern for the potential link between products and pain and they are also concerned about whether or not consumers will accept such advertising (Eridani, 2001). Nevertheless advertising's intrusiveness continues unabated as advertisers desperately seek an audience by whatever means available.

Undercover marketing is growing as a means to get the message directly to the consumer where he or she "lives." In one version, attractive and highly gregarious "commercial kamikazes" are sent into local bars to talk up a particular brand of bottled water.

As it has become ever harder to reach people between the ages of 12 and 34, advertisers have pushed viral marketing entirely underground, pitching them on the sly and hoping that the message takes and spreads, virus-like, with none of the intended marks knowing the better. This might mean leaving cigarette packs in bars, as tobacco companies have done, or loaning automobiles to "key influencers," as Ford did in 1999, when it placed the Ford Focus with 120 people in five major markets. ("Buy me," 2001: 21)

In a rather unique twist on the undercover marketing theme, two young men bound for college convinced First USA, a credit card company, to make them their spokespersons. In exchange for a $40,000 payment to each (they are attending different colleges in California), the two will place First USA logos on their clothing and sports equipment, like surf boards. They will informally spread the word about First USA, and they will conduct formal presentations about managing your money while in college (Zernike, 2001).

UNCERTAINTY IN THE MARKETPLACE

The continual reinvention of advertising through the development of new forms and use of new media signifies uncertainty in the marketplace and how unsure advertisers are of their ability to move the excesses of production through the marketplace via a relatively benign form of communication. Ang (1996) said, "In this sense, it would be mistaken to see the (audience) acting out of difference unambiguously as an act of resistance; what needs to be emphasized, rather, is that the desire to be different can be simultaneously complicit with and defiant against the institutionalization of excess of desire in capitalist postmodernity" (179). She added this is "the chaos that emanates from the institutionalization of infinite semiosis" (179). In other words, the consumer's experience of the hyper-real and hyper-ritualized world of national consumer goods advertising is marked by chaos.[2] In order to understand the work advertising does in the culture and the work we do with it, we have to go beyond issues of consumer resistance and complicity and the chaos that is part of institutionalized excess to see the dynamic as a problematic interaction between consumers and advertisers.

Effects-oriented theories of advertising, which are largely reductionist, do not account for uncertainty in the marketplace; indeed they attempt to weed out uncertainty. In order to understand the place of advertising in everyday American life, uncertainty needs to be accommodated. Uncertainty is a fact of postmodern life that in the context of advertising needs to be viewed in a positive manner. The continuum of meaning that I have described accommodates uncertainty as it recognizes the variability of the "text" of advertising and the range of reactions toward and experiences with advertising. Capitalist postmodernity "is a thoroughly paradoxical place, unified yet multiple, totalized yet deeply unstable, closed and open-ended at the same time" (163). Ang described this communication system as chaotic "where uncertainty is a built-in feature" (163).

Uncertainty is a necessary correlate to the construction of meaning. As Ang said, "communicative practices do not necessarily have to arrive at common meanings at all" (167). When we view the myriad ways in which individuals twist and turn the content of advertising and sometimes choose to reintegrate some of that content for use in their everyday lives, we can see advertising as part of the dynamic of human interaction. Within this construct communication is no longer the central focus, but is part of the social and cultural, and because meaning is determined through the variety and range of possible social interactions it is indeterminate.

INDETERMINACY OF MEANING

The concept of *indeterminate meanings* suggests that the circuit between sender, message, and receiver is not closed. Such a circuit of communication is based on a linear connection between the sender and receiver, however the connection is more complex. The dynamic relationship between consumer and advertiser within a chaotic structure of communication is more matrix-like, where energy is exerted and expended through resistance and complicity. Within such a multidimensional matrix, advertisers, as purveyors of not just products and services, but of meaning and experience as well, maintain their hegemonic ability to convey ideology. An advertising system based on indeterminate meanings is more complex when seen within the social contexts of everyday life. Within the complexity of social relations it is not just advertisers and audiences that work within a simple dialectic or circuit, but advertising working within the social contexts and relationships of audiences. It is these dynamic forces both—intrapersonal and interpersonal—that have been revealed to contain the social practices of resistance and complicity. Ang (1996) supported the need to "think about the relation of power and meaning in more multidimensional terms, to reorganize the operation of multiple forms of power at different points in the system of social networks in which both 'senders' (e.g., media) and 'receivers' (e.g., audiences) are complexly located and produce meanings" (169). The difficulty is in resisting closure as it does not allow for "unresolved ambiguity and contradiction" within the uncertainty of meaning construction.

A condition for living in the postmodern capitalist culture is "free-yet-bounded-ness" (170). This is reminiscent of de Certeau's (1984) notion of "escaping without leaving." This view toward social practices in everyday life acknowledges the power of advertisers, but recognizes the difficulty of locating the structures of power or resistance. It is apparent that we operate within a cultural container. But the matrix is multidimensional with layers of power, resistance and complicity. Within these layers are "cracks" that de Certeau described as the tactics—tricks and games—that allow one to use advertising to subvert the dominant system and create new spaces. Consumers participate in the creation of culture as they seek to escape the boundaries laid before them by consumptive capitalism. This is the mercantile carnival transformed by postmodern society. And, as Fiske (1989) pointed out, we are not necessarily escaping from anything in particular, but are escaping to something that is relevant; in the process we may push the edge of the boundaries.

Generally speaking, postmodern society is characterized by uncertainty. What critical theory has to come to terms with " is not certainty of (and wholesale opposition to) the spread of a culturally coherent capitalist modernity, but the uncertainty brought about by the disturbing incoherence of a globalized capitalist postmodernity, and the mixture of resistance and complicity occurring within it" (Ang, 1996: 171). The ethnographic methods used in the research for Part II of this book described how the bottom–top, micro-powers of audience activity are both complicit with and resistant to the dominant, macro-forces within capitalist postmodernity.

The variety and range of responses to advertisements appear as complicity and resistance, and may be rooted in the dynamic social structure that undergirds the use of advertising in everyday life. The focus of this book has been the everyday life activities in which advertising use exists. In particular, this book has been concerned with the "cracks" in the wall through which individuals contribute to the creation of culture. This is the uncontrolled space in which consumers find ways to reintegrate advertising texts into their everyday lives. The theory presented here privileges everyday life, beyond the sender and receiver, to include the multiple contexts—intrapersonal and interpersonal—that are a part of the dynamic multiple relationships that exist within everyday life. Power in this sense is not merely between the media and the audience, but between the media, audience and with whomever else the audience member interacts as a part of their everyday life. Power not only exists between advertisers and audiences, it also exists between the individuals who comprise those audiences— autonomous players in the game of advertising. At some point or points in the course of daily life advertising or elements thereof may become intertwined. To this end Ang (1996) suggested that indeterminacy of meaning is the product of "too many unpredictable determinations" (172).

The variety and range of uses of advertising that I have described and interpreted "represent the infinite play of differences which makes all identities and all meanings precarious and unstable," and it is the "infinite play of differences in the site of the social" where we can see culture at work (172). Therefore, the goal should not be to demarcate advertising's boundaries, as meanings will always be in excess of what we limit through the concept of society. In practice, rather than demarcate boundaries, the goal is to locate those spaces where the boundaries have been exceeded—this is where culture is created. We can view resistance and complicity at work as individuals through routine social interaction destroy boundaries and create new space and meaning. It is the social interaction within the context of everyday life that is the site of this struggle.

In the beginning of the 21st century there are myriad opportunities for individuals to consume media and their excessiveness. Among them are 24-hour global networks, an abundance of cable channels, Tivo and Replay TV, and similar technological innovations that allow the viewer to block out the commercials. The ubiquity of the screen through convergence of technologies, like the personal computer and TV, aid advertising as its growing subtlety finds its way into every corner of everyday life. Ang (1996) claimed

> All this can surely only make for an endless, unruly and uncontrollable play of differences in social practices related to television viewing: continuous social differentiation bordering on chaos. . . . But it is precisely this chaos which I suggest we need to take into consideration in understanding the logic of power relations in capitalist postmodernity. (174)

Ironically, it is those chaotic connections that bind us as a culture, not communication as Carey would have us believe.

ADVERTISING AS POSTMODERN CARNIVAL

This variability and range of advertising use in everyday life is not good news for advertisers as they are interested in knowing (and controlling) who is watching, reading, listening and surfing, and controlling the context of their consumption. All of their efforts in this promotional mix are an effort to control the marketplace through a postmodern carnival of sorts. However, consumers have become quite media savvy in their tactics and employ highly developed skills that I referred to as practiced avoidance. But avoidance is not about inattention or escaping without leaving. Rather, in contemporary society we multi-task; we may be in essence in two places at once. Today individuals may split their attention as they, for example, read a magazine or the newspaper while simultaneously looking up to watch the television. Or they listen to music while surfing the Internet. Or in another twist, one can read a magazine while running a magic wand across a bar code that will connect the reader to an advertiser's Web site. The cable news network CNN, among others, simultaneously scrolls the latest news across the bottom of the screen as a news anchor or reporter provides visual news coverage. In a similar vein, talking on a cellular phone while driving is a form of split attention. And in yet another form, as this book has demonstrated, consumers may engage in reverie while consuming advertising. This is partially a function of the multitude of media and channels available, and the technology that lets consumers, for example, watch two television stations at once (picture-in-picture). Beyond the technology, consumers have developed elaborate practices to negotiate their way through the media jungle.

Beyond these uses of technology, advertising continually encourages consumers to remake themselves and their lives. The need for "newer," "bigger," "faster," and "better" are part of a system of planned obsolescence that constantly calls on consumers to wallow in the excess that advertising presents. Ang (1996) maintained, "capitalist postmodernity's 'true realm of uncertainty' has to do with the system's ambiguous stance towards the infinitude of the social itself: as much as it wants to control it, it also depends on exploiting it" (176). Dynamic perpetual change is a characteristic of consumption capitalism of which advertising stimulates the excessiveness of the social and excess of desire that results in the unpredictability of meaning and identity. "In other words, at the heart of capitalist postmodernity is an extreme contradiction: on the one hand, its very operation depends on encouraging infinite semiosis, but, on the other hand, like every systemic order, it cannot let infinite semiosis go totally unchecked" (177).

Resistance and complicity to advertising may unsettle the boundaries of the system, but they do not destroy those boundaries— social practices are limited within the parameters of the culture. Hegemony is still at work; it is just made more complex. In their attempt to make certain what is uncertain, advertisers spend enormous sums on research that is ultimately wasteful when viewed within the construct of chaos in which infinite semiosis operates. Within this cultural system advertisers can retain their hegemonic power, but the way they exercise that power is uncertain. Because of this inherent contradiction, advertisers are hard pressed to manage and order everyday existence. Nevertheless, in a world of seamless advertising the never-ending cat and mouse game goes on. The postmodern carnival of advertising conjures up a false world, one that lacks authenticity. When individuals reintegrate elements of advertising into their everyday lives they, in a sense, attempt to breathe life into the false or flattened world that is presented. Individuals in U.S. society in this sense try to make the inauthentic quality of advertising into an authentic or quasi-authentic experience.

Recall is the standard measure of advertising effectiveness. However, we often are not able to recall ads and when we do recall them sometimes we confuse the contents of the text. That is to say we cannot connect a catch phrase or slogan to the correct company or product and visa versa. But that failure should not be taken as advertising's ineffectiveness. The imaginary social world of the individual is not part of the recall measure or any other evaluative criteria for that matter utilized by the industry, nor do advertisers track the other ways in which they impact the culture, like when a catch phrase or slogan for a period of time enters into everyday speech and the infinite variations of its use. Nevertheless these are ways in which advertising impacts the culture and are ways we create culture. One industry response is to make advertisements more entertaining. Another response is to make advertising even more fully ingrained into everyday life. In this sense, we no longer have to worry about recall if the advertisement or product is continually before us. The advertisement becomes disengaged from the product and conversely the product becomes disengaged from the advertisement, but the sell, no matter how subtle, is still there.

Meaning cannot derive from a single advertisement in the same way that meaning is not derived from any single object. Meaning is part of the whole—a gestalt. In this sense, you cannot isolate the sofa from the rest of the furniture in the living room. Ultimately, from a cultural perspective, it does not matter whether we arrest meaning from the advertisement correctly or incorrectly. Failing the "reading test" at first glance affects the purveyor or marketer of goods who wants to convey consistent and reliable information. And of course an incorrect reading of an advertisement may bear responsibility for failed sales, if one wants to use that as a measure of an advertisement's success. Failing the reading test or getting the message wrong is merely a part of an imperfect system. The value of advertising are embedded in the consumption of advertising that is manifested in the ways in which we use its content in our everyday lives.

ENDNOTES

1. *The Runner* was cancelled before it aired because its content and structure in which individuals attempt to cross the country undetected made network executives uncomfortable in light of the September 11 disaster.
2. By chaos I do not mean disruption or disorder. Chaos refers to a theory that suggests that order, balance, and equilibrium are complicated by external and internal instabilities. The conditions of moving equilibrium suggest the disorderly nature of the advertising system may move from equilibrium to a far from equilibrium state, and the system may be stable and unstable at the same time. For information on Chaos theory see Gleick (1987). An application of chaos theory to modern American Fiction can be found in Slethaug (2000).

APPENDIX

NOTES ON METHODOLOGY

The diversity of research perspectives within the field of communication lends itself to multidisciplinary approaches to the study of advertising. Because the primary emphasis of this book is cultural, both traditional and alternative research methodologies were employed. The humanistic approaches described in this appendix are well suited to gain access to the meaningful ways in which individuals utilize advertising that are perhaps obscure and taken for granted. As the focus of the book is on the particularities of everyday life, it was important to see advertising at work in natural environments that consider human activity and interaction during and outside of commercial media consumption.

Garfinkel (1967) defined *ethnomethodology* as the investigation of "artful practices of everyday life" (11). An ethnological study of the ways advertising is experienced as a part of everyday life requires an examination of the ways in which individuals reintegrate the content of advertising within their daily routines, what I referred to in this book as *social practices*.

The task of studying advertising in naturalistic settings in the context of everyday life can be a frustrating one. When I undertook this project the idea of where to find advertising within naturalistic settings was somewhat daunting. And the bigger challenge regarded how to access individuals' fantasies, daydreams, and dreams. One cannot simply and directly ask people to reveal their fantasies, daydreams, dreams, and other sensitive information about imaginary social relationships. In other words, people cannot stream or fantasize on demand. Not only is such material potentially embarrassing, it is terribly mundane. With regard to the latter, people generally are not aware that they engage in such an inner world of imaginative activity. After all, advertising is something most people take for granted, and they are not readily aware of their use of advertising in everyday life.

The research questions I was asking did not lend themselves to traditional methods of study. And although this research is not holistic, that is to say, I have not covered all of the uses of advertising in everyday life, I do think that through the various methods detailed here I have captured enough of it to draw some interesting conclusions and to develop some theoretical considerations. Some of the larger questions I had to deal with were as follow: "Where do you find advertising used in everyday life?" "How broad or narrow is its use?" "In what contexts are advertising uses likely to emerge?" "How do you go beyond the kinds of responses likely garnered from traditional questionnaires?" "How do you go about, in a sensitive manner, listening to the conversations of family, friends, neighbors, colleagues and strangers who are dispersed across so many venues?" The goal was to get as close to the phenomenon of advertising use as I could. I wanted to see how advertising was used during media consumption and in social contexts outside of media consumption, and I wanted to delve deeply inside informants' imaginary worlds, including their stream of consciousness, fantasies, dreams, and imaginary relationships, to investigate the ways in which advertising might be present.

Rather than working within predefined categories, the methods utilized in the research are meant to illuminate how advertising is utilized in the context of everyday American life. To that end, Carey (1975) wrote, "A cultural science of communication then views human behavior or more accurately human action, as a text. Our task is to construct a sequence of symbols—speech, writing, and gesture—that contain interpretations. Our task, like that of a literary critic, is to interpret the interpretations" (173). For example, Pacanowsky and Anderson (1982) found that because ethnographic methods are "concerned with revealing 'realities' embedded in social enactments, media use may be construed as part of the structure of some transaction" (743). Media content may be used subsequent to media consumption in a variety of social constructions, each of which defines the use (gives it purpose) within that particular social structure. Uses, created after one attends to the media, are implicit in one's social constructions and are behaviorally embedded as well as symbolically manifested.

Storey (1999) said "The nature and extent of impact a text will have on its consumer cannot be judged by formal analysis alone; the only way to decide this question is by examining how it is made meaningful by its consumers" (32).

Ethnography (including what passes for ethnography in cultural studies) does not of course give direct access to why and how people consume and turn particular commodities into culture. What it does provide access to is people's accounts of what they are doing and why they do it? This means, regardless of descriptive accuracy that ethnographic accounts are always reports on other people's reports of what they do and why they do it. (33)

It is the researcher's task, then, to interpret the use from the social structure and describe it. The interpretive framework is based on the work of Geertz who suggested, "meanings are not 'in people's heads' but are shared and public" (in Caughey, 1982: 223). Attention is placed on "thick description" of social discourse, the symbols and rituals through which meanings are sustained. Geertz stated:

To grasp concepts which, for another people, are experience-near, and to do so well enough to place them in illuminating connection with those experience-distant concepts that theorists have fashioned to capture the general features of social life, is clearly a task at least as delicate, if a bit less magical, as putting oneself into someone else's skin. The trick is not to achieve some inner correspondence of spirit with your informants; preferring, like the rest of us, to call their souls their own, they are not going to be altogether keen about such an effort anyhow. The trick is to figure out what the devil they think they are up to. (482)

The methodological question raised by Geertz concerns "searching out and analyzing the symbolic forms—words, images, institutions, behaviors—in terms of which, in each place, people actually represent themselves to themselves and to one another" (483).

For Fiske (1987), the value of the ethnography in Morley's studies of television viewers

lies in its shift of emphasis away from the textual and ideological construction of the subject to socially and historically situation of people. It (Ethnography) reminds us that actual people in actual situations watch and enjoy actual television programs. It acknowledges the differences between people despite their social construction, and pluralizes theories that stress the singularity of television's meanings and its reading subjects. It enables us to account for diversity both within the social formation and within the processes of culture. (63)

Writing about ethnography and the study of television viewing Fiske said:

The object of ethnographic study is the way people live their culture. Its value for us lies in its shift of emphasis away from the textual and ideological construction of the subject to socially and historically situated people. It reminds us that actual people in actual situations watch and enjoy actual television programs. It acknowledges the differences between people despite their social construction, and pluralizes the meanings and pleasures that they find in television. It thus contradicts theories that stress the singularity of television's meanings and its reading subjects. It enables us to account for diversity both within the social formation and within the process of culture. (63)

I utilized multiple methods as they were deemed appropriate and I utilized techniques within those methods that may have varied from traditional approaches with regard to analysis and interpretation. As I collected data, I would look for emergent patterns that provide confirmation for the phenomena I was studying. The following provides the specific details of data collection used for the research included in this book.

The individuals whom I studied do not constitute a representative sample, nor was this the goal. The informants for all this research were individuals who lived in the planned community of Columbia, Maryland. These studies also involved undergraduate and graduate college students at a private college and historically Black state university in the northeast. The ages of my informants ranged from 18 to 55. They were diverse in terms of race, and males and females were both represented in the sample.

CHAPTER 3 – THINKING ABOUT ADVERTISING: MAKING, UNMAKING, AND REMAKING MEANING

In researching the kinds of stream of consciousness and fantasy behavior people engaged in while consuming commercial media I was faced with a major dilemma. How do you get inside informants' heads to render their thoughts and fantasies transparent? I was interested in gathering information at the point of intersection—when the individual was consuming media, during this routine practice of everyday life. Direct observation would not lend itself to such an end. Following the approach advocated by Caughey (1984), informants were asked to "engage in retrospective observations in natural social settings just after a stream has spontaneously occurred" (122). Informants were instructed to catch themselves during routine moments of media consumption and to identify what they had just been thinking about. They wrote down as complete a record as they could, tracing the sequence back as far as possible. Using this technique, most people can produce detailed accounts of their reverie. Caughey suggested that in this sense, "Informants can be enlisted as co-ethnographers and asked to report on their own memory of their own experience immediately after the experience has occurred" (25).

In order to avoid coercing information to create the stream, a number of steps were taken. First, informants consumed media in naturalistic settings (e.g., watching television or reading a magazine at home). Second, they recorded their thoughts over a 2-week period. This provided an extensive record of their streaming activity. Third, 150 episodes from the self-reports were grouped together into emergent patterns. Working with these episodes, patterns of memories and anticipations emerged through the self-talk of informants.

CHAPTER 4 – DREAMING, DREAM SHARING, AND ADVERTISING

Like the stream of consciousness, dreams are not observable to the outsider. One has to rely on the individual to recount the dream. In order to examine the presence of media figures in dreams, this research utilized both a dream questionnaire and individual dream reports. The questionnaire was administered to 241 undergraduate college students. Informants were asked how often they dreamed and how often they recalled their dreams. Responses to these questions were framed in Likert format, with responses *just about every night, a couple of times a week, maybe once a week, occasionally,* and *never.* Several questions specifically addressed media presence in dreams: "Have you ever dreamed about a media figure? Please describe." "Have you ever dreamed about a commercial or advertised product or that you were in an advertisement? Please describe." "Have you ever dreamed about a television program or that you were in one? Please describe?" Participants in this research were asked to keep a dream diary for a 2-week period so that at least one fairly complete dream could be produced. Participants were not prompted to produce a media-centered dream. The dreams were content-analyzed based on a set of categories developed by C. Hall and Van De Castle (1966).

This chapter was concerned with two distinct practices— dreams we have about advertising and the sharing of dreams with others. In order to study dream sharing, a questionnaire was constructed to identify the types of dreams people share, the individuals or groups with whom dreams are shared, and the social context in which dreams are shared. This questionnaire asked about remembering dreams: "How often do you recall your dreams?" Informants were asked if they could recall the last time (or one time) when they told someone a dream, and if so, who was the individual. Informants were asked to describe the social situation (context) in which they told the dream and the purpose in telling the dream. They were also asked about the other person's reaction or response to being told the dream and whether this was different from the kind of reaction they had hoped to elicit. Other questions focused on the context and safety of dream sharing, asking informants if they could think of a situation in which it would be unsafe to tell someone about a dream and if so, to describe it. They were also asked if there was a particular kind of dream they would never consider telling anyone and, if so, to describe it. The questionnaire included questions regarding how informants felt upon waking from a dream, whether the "mood" set by the dream affected them during the day, and about cultural referents in dreams such as movies, television, and media figures.

CHAPTER 5 – THE IMAGINARY SOCIAL WORLD AND USE OF MEDIA FIGURES IN ADVERTISING

The study of imaginary social relationships with media figures that appear in advertising does not readily lend itself to direct observation. The experiences to be examined are private; the researcher cannot be present at the social scene looking over the shoulder of the informant. Such imaginary social relationships, however, can be viewed through the informants' self-reflective reports and through ethnographic interviews of their experiences.

Ethnographic interviews were held with a convenience sample of 21 informants. The interviews consisted primarily of open-ended questions about advertising and celebrities. Each interview commenced with a general discussion of advertising and attitudes toward advertising. Informants were then asked to identify media figures that are significant to them, including one who may have appeared in an advertisement. Informants were asked to describe the nature of that relationship and then to describe the role the media figure's appearance in an advertisement might play in the relationship. Informants discussed their large repertoire of celebrity facts and gossip, including facts about the media figure's life, the roles the media figure played, other background information, as well as knowledge of the media figure's appearance in an advertisement.

Additionally, a convenience sample of 70 individuals over a 2-week period developed self-reflective reports of their imaginary social relationships. The self-reports, completed in the privacy of their homes, were similar to a journal or diary, and included entries describing reactions to and interactions with media figures in the context of media consumption. The descriptions of imaginary relationships were not coded into fixed categories. Rather, descriptions of those relationships were interpreted based on emergent patterns regarding the nature of or intensity of the relationship, social or physical attraction and the broader context, including longevity, in which the imaginary relationship existed.

CHAPTER 6 – SOCIAL DISCOURSE AND ADVERTISING AS SOCIAL PRACTICE

The selection of the planned city of Columbia, Maryland (with its mall, "village" shopping centers, schools, public swimming pools, and parks) as the site of the research was dictated by the desire for a wide range of observational opportunities in a compact geographical area. The field investigation took a "scattered" approach with observations taking place at various locations at different times of the day.

Observers included the primary researcher and 12 co-ethnographers. Fieldnotes were collected during a 3-month period. There were 164 observations in naturalistic settings. This type of observation calls for some exercise in judgment as the task was to describe the overt actions of participants during social interactions. All of the advertising references were spontaneous and were part of naturally occurring talk. Consider, for example, the youngster who, while standing at the edge of a public swimming pool about to jump in, makes a public declaration that he is about to take the "Nestea Plunge."

A second part of this research included self-reflective reports of 24 individuals. These informants were asked to keep a journal in which they described their uses (if any) of advertising content in conversations over a 2-week period. Informants were initially prompted with examples to ensure that the "exercise" was clear to them. Two hundred examples of the use of advertising content in the course of everyday conversations were collected.

Additional examples were drawn from an analysis of advertising content as it appeared in print and broadcast media. Print media included The *New York Times, The Wall Street Journal, The Washington Post, The Baltimore Sun, People, New Age Journal, Sports Illustrated, Time, Nation's Business,* and *Advertising Age.* Electronic media included: *ABC's World News Tonight, 60 Minutes, Seinfeld, Friends, That 70s Show,* and *The Drew Carey Show*; and on radio, *The Diane Rehm Show* and *All Things Considered.*

The traditional and alternative methods employed in this research provide a way into the complex processes employed when individuals are confronted by a stimulus—advertising—that is straightforward and purposeful. The variety and range of responses to advertisements become a kind of cultural expression for the individual. And, although the sample utilized in this series of studies is not representative from a statistical point of view, the informants are derived from a wide range of backgrounds. Their responses demonstrate the phenomenon under consideration in each of the studies.

REFERENCES

Aaker, D., & Day, G. (1978). *Consumerism: Search for the consumer interest.* New York: Free Press.

Allen, I. (1982). Talking about media experiences: Everyday life as popular culture. *Journal of Popular Culture, 16*(3), 106–115.

Alperstein, N., & Vann, B. (1997). Star gazing: A socio-cultural approach to the study of dreaming about media figures. *Communication Quarterly, 45*(3), 142-152.

Altheide, D., & Snow, R. (1979). *Media logic.* Newbury Park, CA: Sage.

Anderson, J., & Meyer, T. (1987). *Mediated communication: A social action perspective.* Newbury Park, CA: Sage.

Ang, I. (1991). *Desperately seeking the audience.* London: Routledge.

Ang, I. (1996). *Living room wars: Rethinking media audiences for a post-modern world.* London: Routledge.

Ang, I. (1994). Feminist desire and female pleasure. In J. Storey (Ed.), *Cultural theory and popular culture: A reader* (pp. 513-522). London: Harvester Wheatsheaf.

Beaudet, D. (1991). Encountering the monster in children's dreams: Combat, taming, and engulfment. *Quadrant, 24*(1), 65-73.

Belch, G., & Belch, M. (2001). *Advertising and promotion.* New York: McGraw-Hill.

Berger, A. (2000). *Ads, fads and consumer culture: Advertising's impact on American character and society.* Lawham, MD: Rowman & Littlefield.

Berger, C. R. (1985). Uncertain outcome values in predicted relationships: Uncertainty reduction theory then and now. *Human Communication Research, 12*, 34-38.

Berger, C.R., & Calabrese, R. (1975). Some explanations in initial interaction and beyond: Toward a developmental theory of interpersonal communication. *Human Communication Research, 1*, 99-112.

Berger, P., & Luckmann, T. (1966). *The social construction of reality.* New York: Doubleday.

Bogart, L. (1995). *Commercial culture: The media system and the public interest.* New York: Oxford University Press.

Boorstin, D. (1992). *The image: A guide to pseudo-events in America.* New York: Vintage Books. (Original work published 1962)

Buy me. (2001, July 15) *The New York Times Magazine*, p. 21.

Campbell, C. (1987). *The romantic ethic and the spirit of modern consumerism.* Oxford: Basil Blackwell.

Carey, J. (1989). *Communication as culture: Essays on media and society.* Boston: Unwin Hyman.

Carey, J. (1986). The dark continent in American journalism. In R. Manoff & M. Schudson (Eds.), *Reading the news* (pp. 146–196). New York: Pantheon.

Carey, J. (1975). Communication and culture. *Communication Research, 2*(2), 173-191.

Carter, B. (2001, April 30). New reality show planning to put ads between the ads. *The New York Times*, pp. A1, A17.

Caughey, J. (1982). The ethnography of everyday life: Theories and methods for American culture studies. *American Quarterly, 34*(3), 222–243.

Caughey, J. (1984). *Imaginary social worlds.* Lincoln: University of Nebraska Press.

Cornish, P. (1987, November 2). Advertising that gets talked about. *Advertising Age*, p. 64.

Deber, C. (1979). *The pursuit of attention: Power and individualism in everyday life.* London: Oxford University Press.

de Certeau, M. (1984). *The practice of everyday life.* Berkeley: University of California Press.

Douglas, M., & Isherwood, B., (1996). *The world of goods: Towards an anthropology of consumption.* London: Routledge.

Driver, J., & Foxall, G. (1984). *Advertising policy and practice.* London: Holt, Rinehart & Winston.

Eco, U. (1979). *The role of the reader: Exploration in the semiotics of texts.* Bloomington: Indiana University Press.

Eco, U. (1980). Towards a semiotic inquiry into the TV message. In J. Corner & J. Hawthorn (Eds.), *Communication studies: An introductory reader* (pp. 103-126). London: Arnold.

Elkin, T. (2001, April 26). Sony touts new digital technology. *Advertising Age*, p. 41.

Elliot, S. (2001, July, 24). The new president of BBDO North America reflects on life and business in the colonies. *The New York Times*, p. C8.

Emery, E., (1972). *The press and America: An interpretive history of the mass media*. Englewood Cliffs: Prentice-Hall.

Eridani, T. (2001, May 8). Italian hospitals hope to fortify budgets as advertisers find place on premises. *The Wall Street Journal*, p. B7C.

Esslin, M. (1987). Aristotle and the advertisers: The television commercial considered as a form of drama. In H. Newcomb (Ed.), *Television: The critical view* (4th ed., pp. 304-318). New York: Oxford University Press.

Ewen, S. (1988). *All consuming images*. New York: Basic Books.

Ewen, S., & Ewen, E. (1982). *Channels of desire*. New York: McGraw-Hill.

Fairclough, N. (1989). *Language and power*. New York: Longman.

Feshbach, S. (1976). The role of fantasy in response to television. *Journal of Social Issues, 32*(4), 71-85.

Fine, G., & Leighton, L. (1993). Nocturnal omissions: Steps toward a sociology of dreams. *Symbolic Interaction, 16*(2), 95-104.

Fiske, J. (1987). *Television culture*. London: Routledge.

Fiske, J. (1989). *Understanding popular culture*. Boston: Unwin Hyman.

Fortini-Campbell, L. (2001). *Hitting the sweet spot*. Chicago: The Copy Workshop.

Fowles, J. (1996). *Advertising and popular culture*. Thousand Oaks, CA: Sage.

Fox, S. (1984). *The mirror makers: A history of American advertising and its creators*. New York: Vintage Books.

Gamson, J. (1994). *Claims to fame: Celebrity in contemporary America*. Berkeley: University of California Press.

Garfinkle, H. (1967). *Studies in ethnomethodology*. Englewood Cliffs, NJ: Prentice-Hall.

Geertz, C. (1973). *The interpretation of cultures*. New York: Basic Books.

Gillespie, M. (1995). *Television, ethnicity and cultural change*. London: Routledge.

Gitlin, T. (1993). Flat and happy. *The Wilson Quarterly, 27*(4), 47-55.

Gleick, J. (1987). *Chaos: Making a new science*. New York: Penguin Books.

Glenn, P., & Knapp, M. (1987). The interactive framing of play in adult conversations. *Communication Quarterly, 35*(1), 48–66.

Goffman, I. (1959). *The presentation of self in everyday life*. New York: Anchor Books.

Goffman, I. (1976). *Gender advertisements*. New York: Harper and Row.

Goldman, K (1994, January 7). Dead celebrities are resurrected as pitchmen. *The Wall Street Journal*, pp. B1, 2.

Gornstein, L. (2001, February 27). Joe Isuzu ad character back from marketing scrap heap. Associated Press.

Gottdiener, M. (2000). *New forms of consumption*. Lanham, MD: Rowman & Littlefield.

Gramsci, A. (1998). Hegemony, intellectuals and the state. In J. Storey (Ed.), *Cultural theory and popular culture: A reader* (pp. 210-216). Essey: Pearson Education.

Grossberg, L. (1997). Wandering audiences, nomadic critics. In *Bringing it all back home: Essays on cultural studies*. Durham, Duke University Press.

Hall, C., & Van De Castle, R. (1966). *The content analysis of dreams*. New York: Appleton-Century-Croft.

Hall, S. (1980). Culture studies: Two paradigms. *Media, Culture and Society, 2*, 57-72.

Horton, D., and Wohl, R. (1956). Mass communication and para-social interaction: Observations on intimacy at a distance. *Psychiatry, 19*, 215-229.

Jamieson, K., & Campbell, K. (2001). *The interplay of influence*. Belmont, CA: Wadsworth.

James, N. C., & McCain, T. (1982), Television games preschool children play: Patterns, themes and uses. *Journal of Broadcasting, 26*(4), 783–800.

Jhally, S. (1989). Advertising as religion: The dialectic of technology and magic. In I. Angus & S. Jhally (Eds.), *Cultural politics in contemporary America* (pp. 217-229). New York: Routledge.

Joseph, W. B. (1982). The credibility of physically attractive communicators: A review. *Journal of Advertising, 11*(3), 15-24.

Jowett, G., & Linton, J. (1980). *Movies as mass communication*. Beverly Hills, CA: Sage.

Klapp, O. (1964). *Symbolic leaders: Public dramas and public men*. Chicago: Aldine.

Klinger, E. (1971). *Structure and function of fantasy*. New York: Wiley.

Klinger, E., Gregoire, K., & Barta, S. (1973). Psychological correlates of mental activity: Eye movements, alpha, and heart rate during suppression, concentration, search, and choice. *Psychophysiology, 10*, 471-477

Krugman, H. (1988). Point of view: Limits of attention of advertising. *Journal of Advertising Research, 28*(5), 49.

Kubey, R., & Csikszentmihalyi, M. (1990). *Television and the quality of life: How viewing shapes everyday experience*. Mahwah, NJ: Erlbaum.

Langer, J. (1981). Television's personality system. *Media Culture and Society, 4*, 351-365.

Lavidge, R., & Steiner, G. (1961, October). A model for predictive measurements of advertising effectiveness. *Journal of Marketing, 24,* 59-62.

Lears, J. (1994). *Fables of abundance: A cultural history of advertising in America.* New York: Basic Books.

Lefton, T. (2001, June 11). Zapped out? Try "virtual placement." *Newsweek,* p. 560.

Leiss, W., Kline, S., & Jhally, S. (1986). *Social communication in advertising: Persons, products, and images of well-being.* New York: Methuen.

Levy, M. (1979). Watching television as para-social interaction. *Journal of Broadcasting, 23,* 69-80.

Lewis, J. (1994). The meaning of things: Audiences, ambiguity, and power. In J. Cruz & J. Lewis (Eds.), *Viewing, reading, listening: Audiences and cultural reception* (pp. 19-32). Boulder, CO: Westview Press.

Lull, J. (1980). The social uses of television. *Human Communication Research, 6*(3), 197-209.

Marra, J. (1990). *Connective thinking: Techniques for generating advertising ideas.* Englewood Cliffs, NJ: Prentice-Hall.

Marriot, M. (2001, August 30). Playing with consumers: With online advertising not living up to expectations, companies turn to games to pitch their products. *The New York Times,* p. E1.

McAllister, M. (1996). *The commercialization of American culture: New advertising control and democracy.* Thousand Oaks, CA: Sage.

McCracken, G. (1987). Advertising: Meaning or information. In M. Wallendorf & P. Anderson (Eds.), *Advances in consumer research* (Vol. 14, pp. 121-124). Provo, UT: Association for Consumer Research.

Meyers, G. (1994). *Words in ads.* London: Edward Arnold.

Meyers, G. (1999). *Ad worlds.* London: Oxford University Press.

Mick, D. (1987). Toward a semiotic of advertising story grammars. In J. Umiker–Sebeok (Ed.), *Marketing and semiotics* (pp. 249–278). New York: Mouton de Gruyter.

Miller, D. (1987). *Material culture and mass consumption.* Oxford: Basil Blackwell.

Morris, M. (1992). On the beach. In L. Grossberg, C. Nelson, & P. Treichler (Eds.), *Cultural studies* (pp. 181-209). London and New York: Routledge.

Moscovici, S. (1981). On social representations. In J. Forgas (Ed.), *Social cognition: Perspectives on everyday understanding* (pp. 181–209). London: Academic Press.

Mullan, B. (1997). *Consuming television: Television and its audience.* Oxford: Blackwell.

Pacanowsky, M., & Anderson, J. (1982). Cop talk and media use. *Journal of Broadcasting, 26*(4), 741–756.

Packard, V. (1957). *Hidden persuaders.* New York: Pocket Books.

Palmer, P. (1986). *The lively audience: A study of children around the TV set.* Boston: Allen & Unwin.

Plummer, J. (1971). A theoretical view of advertising communication. *Journal of Communication, 21,* 315-325.

Potter, D. (1954). *People of plenty: Economic abundance and the American character.* Chicago: University of Chicago Press.

Radway, J. (1998). Reception study: Ethnography and the problems of dispersed audiences and nomadic subjects. *Cultural Studies, 2*(3), 359-367.

Radway, J. (1991). Interpretive communities and variable literacies: The functions of romance reading. In C. Murkerji & M. Schudson (Eds.), *Rethinking popular culture: Contemporary perspectives in cultural studies* (pp. 465-486). Berkeley: University of California Press.

Reeves, J. (1987). Television stars: The case for Mr. T. In H. Newcomb (Ed.), *Television: The critical view* (4th ed., pp. 445-454). New York: Oxford University Press.

Real, M. (1977). *Mass mediated culture.* Englewood, NJ: Prentice-Hall.

Reid, L., & Frazer, C. (1980). Television at play. *Journal of Communication, 30,* 66–73.

Rook, D. (1985). The ritual dimension of consumer behavior. *Journal of Consumer Research, 12*(3), 251-164.

Rotzoll, K., Haefner, J., & Sandage, C. (1976). *Advertising in contemporary society: Perspectives toward understanding.* Columbus, OH: Southwestern.

Rubin, V., Mayer, C., & Friedman, H. (1982). The performance of company president versus spokesperson in television commercials. *Journal of Advertising Research, 22*(4), 31-33.

Scannell, P. (1998). Media—language—world. In A. Bell & P. Garret (Eds.), *Approaches to media discourse* (pp. 251-267). Walden, MA: Blackwell.

Schickel, R. (1985). *Intimate strangers: The culture of celebrity.* New York: Doubleday.

Schudson, M. (1984). *Advertising, the uneasy persuasion: Its dubious impact on American society.* New York: Basic Books.

Schwartz, T. (1974). *The responsive chord.* New York: Anchor.

Shannon, B. (1990). Why are dreams cinematographic? *Metaphor and Symbolic Activity, 5*(4), 235-248.

Sherry, Jr., J. (1987). Advertising as a cultural system. In J. Umiker–Sebeck (Ed.), *Marketing and semiotics* (pp. 441-461). New York: Mouton de Gruyter.

Silverstone, R. (1994). *Television and everyday life.* London: Routledge.

Sivulka, J. (1998). *Soap, sex, and cigarettes: A cultural history of American advertising.* Belmont, CA: Wadsworth.

Slethaug, G. (2000). *Beautiful chaos: Chaos theory and metachaotics in recent American fiction.* Albany: State University of New York Press.

Snow, R. (1988). Forms, formats, and grammatical structure in mass media. In D. Mains & C. Couch (Eds.), *Communication and social structure* (pp. 201-214). Chicago: Charles Thomas.

Solomon, M. (1983). The role of products as social stimuli: A symbolic interactionism perspective. *Journal of Consumer Research, 10,* 319-329.

Stephenson, W. (1967). *The play theory of mass communication.* Chicago: University of Chicago Press.

Storey, J. (1993). *Cultural theory and popular culture.* Athens: University of Georgia Press.

Storey, J. (1999). *Cultural consumption and everyday life.* New York: Oxford University Press.

Sunnafrank, M. (1986). Predicted outcome value during initial interactions: A reformulation of uncertainty reduction theory. *Human Communication Research, 12,* 3-33.

Tedlock, B. (1992). *Dreaming: Anthropological and psychological interpretations.* Santa Fe, NM: School of American Research Press.

Terkel, S. (1995). *Life on the screen: Identity in the age of the Internet.* New York: Simon & Schuster.

Till, B., & Shimp, T. (1998). Endorsers in advertising: The case of negative celebrity information. *Journal of Advertising, 27*(1), 67-82.

Toynbee, A. (1964). *America and the world revolution.* New York: Oxford University Press.

Tsui, B. (2001, February 5). Bowl poll: Ads don't mean sales. *Advertising Age,* p. 1, 33.

Twitchell, J. (1996). *AdCult USA.* New York: Columbia University Press.

Twitchell, J. (2000). *Twenty ads that shook the world.* New York: Crown.

Van De Castle, R. (1994). *Our dreaming mind.* New York: Ballantine.

Vann, B., & Alperstein, N. (1994). *The social utility of dreaming.* Paper presented at the annual conference of the Association for the Study of Dreams, Leiden, The Netherlands.

Vann, B., & Alperstein, N. (2000). *Dream sharing as social interaction.* Dreaming, *10*(2), 111-120.

Veblen, T. (1973). *The theory of the leisure class.* Boston, MA: Houghton Mifflin.

Wallace, A. (1972). Driving to work. In J. Spradely (Ed.), *Culture and cognition: Rules, maps, and plans* (pp. 310-326). San Francisco: Chandler.

Williams, R. (1991). The dream world of mass consumption. In C. Mujkerji & M. Schudson (Eds.), *Rethinking popular culture:*

Contemporary perspectives in cultural studies (pp. 198-235). Berkeley: University of California Press.

Williams, R. (1980). *Problems in materialism and culture: Selected essays.* London: NLB.

Williamson, J. (1991). *Decoding advertisements.* New York: Marion Boyars.

Winship, J. (1987). *Inside women's magazines.* London: Pandora.

Wood, P. (1979). Television as dream. In H. Newcomb (Ed.), *Television: The critical view* (2nd ed., pp. 517-535). New York: Oxford University Press.

Zeitlin, S. (1979). Pop lore: The aesthetic principles in celebrity gossip. *Journal of American Culture, 2*(2), 186-192.

Zernike, K. (2001, July 19). 2 spokesguys pause for a word about their college sponsor. *The New York Times,* p. A22.

AUTHOR/SUBJECT INDEX

Printed in the United States
1200100007B/134

9 781572 735132